B E R N [illegible] I

ALL HIS WORKS FROM [illegible] WORLD

edited by

Andrea Zanella

Fratelli Palombi Editori

INDEX

ISBN 88-7621-780-0

Designed and edited by
Fratelli Palombi Editori

Translation by: Isobel Butters Caleffi

On the cover: G.L. Bernini, *David*, detail.

Gian Lorenzo Bernini

Born in Naples on 7 December 1598, Gian Lorenzo Bernini, embodies the genius of Italian Baroque.
Following in the wake of his father Pietro, a Florentine sculptor, he arrived in Rome in around 1605. From then on until 1680, the year of his death, Gian Lorenzo never left the papal city for long, except in 1665, when he was summoned to Paris by Louis XIV. In the same way, his career, marked by success, underwent only one brief period of gloom during the papacy of Innocent X (1644-1655). Besides being a sculptor, architect, painter, stage designer and playwright, he possessed human qualities not always found in geniuses; charming, and aristocratic in manner, he was ideally suited to life in society. A passionate lover in his youth (his relationship with Costanza Bonarelli, whose portrait he sculpted in 1635, was renowned), he became a good husband and exemplary father in later years.
His formation as a sculptor took place in his father's workshop. Right from a very early age his talent was so exceptional as to attract the attention of cardinal Scipione Borghese, nephew of pope Paul V. It was for the cardinal that he created the statues and groups still now at Galleria Borghese. Also belonging to this period, 1615-1619, are two expressive faces of the *Anima Beata* and *Anima Dannata* and the *St Laurence* [26, 27, 24] of the Contini-Bonacossi Collection.
He enjoyed the unconditional support and admiration of Maffeo Barberini, pope Urban VIII, who entrusted him with the most important commissions of the period.
During the first twenty years of the XVII century Bernini became one of the most highly appreciated sculptors of portraits, among which were those of *Pedro de Foix* (1621), *Carlo Barberini* and *Urban VIII* [25, 33, 31] (both 1630). It was also during this time that, following the wishes of the pope, he began to dedicate himself to painting, a genre which he considered, however, little more than a pastime, but which produced, according to his contemporaries, a conspicuous number of paintings, now mostly lost.
The *Santa Bibiana* [28] made in 1624 for the church of the same name (the restructuring of which he was also responsible for) was the first of a long series of religious statues; these were followed by large monumental works. His most mature artistic output was between 1640 and 1660: he completed the *Tomb of Urban VIII* [66] and created a new type of funeral monument (*Maria Raggi,* 1643, Santa Maria sopra Minerva) but above all he began to think of a work that would unite painting, sculpture and architecture, and which was to be most eloquently expressed in the *Cornaro Chapel* [42, 43, 44, 45] in Santa Maria della Vittoria. During these years he also applied himself to the subject of fountains, his creation of which ranged from the most simple, such as the *Triton Fountain* and the *Fontana delle api* [39, 41],

to the most highly complex, such as the *Fontana del Moro* [38] and in particular the *Four Rivers Fountain* [47, 48, 49], both in Piazza Navona. During this same period he found a way of solving the aesthetic problem of how to hide the traditional plinth used to support busts — by the dynamic use of elaborate drapery, as can be seen in that of *Francesco I d'Este* [50] and produced, with the *Constantine* [70], a new type of equestriam monument that was to be copied throughout the whole period of the Baroque. Between 1655 and 1661 he executed *Daniel* and *Habakkuk* [51, 52] for the Chigi Chapel in Santa Maria del Popolo (which, facing two other statues of Raphaelesque derivation, conveniently provide a comparison of 17th century Baroque sculpture with that of the previous century). From the sixties onwards all his figures are structured differently: the limbs are slimmer, and the drapery of the clothes becomes more sophisticated and expressive, such as in the case of *Mary Magdalen* [55] here the two strips of folds wind around her body and emphasise the saint's passion, or in the *Angels* [59, 60] for Ponte Sant'Angelo (now in Sant'Andrea delle Fratte).

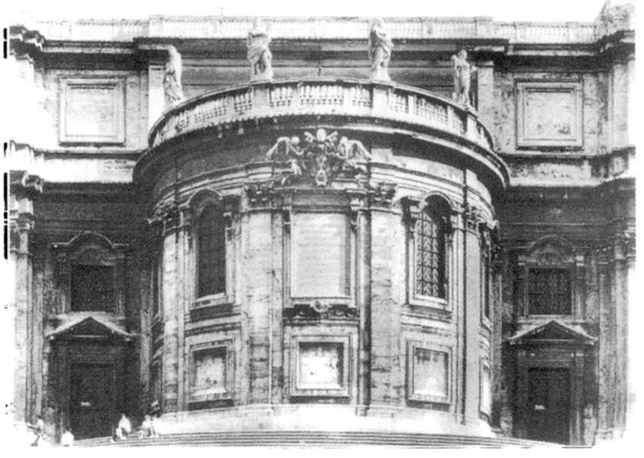

Abside, exterior, 1669 Rome, Church of Santa Maria Maggiore

At the beginning of the seventies, Bernini accentuates his tendency for expressiveness: to increase the emotional tension and the pathos he uses the usual compositional devices, but with greater severity; the bodies become more contracted and the fluid lines of the drapery now become a broken line, as can be seen for example in the *Blessed Ludovica Albertoni* and the *Gabriele Fonseca* [62, 63].

Sensitive to the trends of his time, Bernini during his last years turned to a less expressive and more classical language. These were difficult years for the arts and offers of work did not abound even for geniuses.

Bernini the architect

Nominated "architect of St. Peter's" by Urban VIII in 1629, after the death of Maderno, Bernini carried out various projects including churches and palaces. In 1624 he restored and completed the church of Santa Bibiana in Rome, but essentially his careeer as an architect began with the central elevation of *Palazzo Barberini* [32], of which Maderno had already built the side wings.

The Roman palaces in which Bernini was sooner or later involved

include *Montecitorio* and the so-called *Propaganda Fide* [29] where he was responsible for the facade.
In 1664, not long before his journey to Paris, Bernini drew up plans for the renovation of *Palazzo Chigi* [57] (altered later in the XVIII century when it passed into the hands of the Odescalchi family) in piazza Santi Apostoli, whose facade separated by giant pilasters which rest on the ground floor elevation between two simple rusticated receding wings, became the model for aristrocratic Baroque palaces, not only in Italy. Regarding Bernini's religious architecture, a mention can be made of *Sant'Andrea al Quirinale* [54], small and finely proportioned; the curved lines of the portico and steps blend harmoniously with the great corner pilaster strips and classical pediment and link it to Santa Bibiana, the first of his architectural works executed in 1624.
The elliptical ground plan is reminiscent of the Pantheon and is surmounted by a cupola, richly decorated with polychrome and stuccoes.
The *oeuvre,* however, most closely associated with Bernini's name is the vast *St. Peter's square* [68, 69].

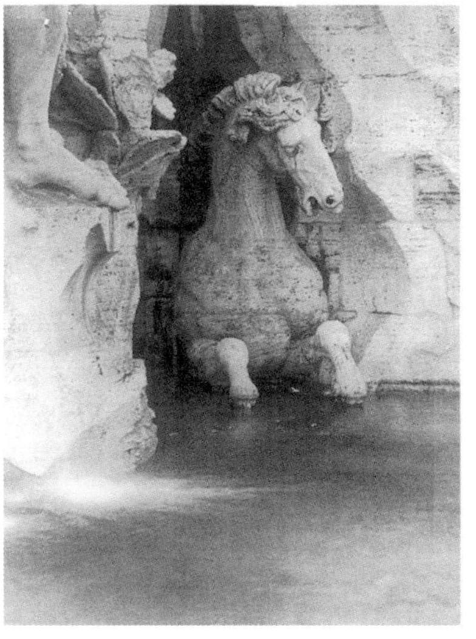

Four Rivers Fountain, detail
1648-1651
travertine and marble

Suggestions for a Bernini itinerary

Although Bernini's works are scattered all over the world, any "Bernini" itinerary must inevitably start in Rome, and take into account three fundamental points of the city: Galleria Borghese, the Vatican and Santa Maria della Vittoria.
It is because of this that here mention is made of the works at Galleria Borghese and the Vatican. Santa Maria della Vittoria is represented here in the photographs of the famous *Ecstasy of St. Teresa* in the Cornaro chapel [42, 43, 44, 45].
Bernini's dream to unite the three arts is realized here, where the role of painting is carried out by the light which colours in differing ways the surfaces it touches.

Galleria Borghese

The group of works conserved in the Galleria Borghese give us a good, if not entirely complete, idea of Bernini's early work. Here are conserved the small group of works executed by the artist for his first important patron, cardinal Scipione Borghese; the oldest of the group

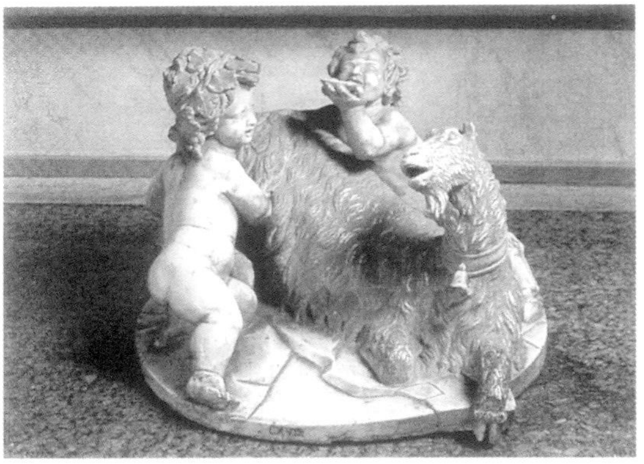

is *Jupiter and the goat Amalthea,* where he imitates classical art to perfection and indeed improves on the Hellenistic models from which he takes inspiration. The *Aeneas, Anchises and Ascanius* [11], perhaps executed in collaboration with his father, shows us in its winding composition, a Bernini still tied to Mannerist sculpture. The *David* [18, 19], on the other hand, has broken away completely from this and demonstrates the revolutionary substance of the whole of Bernini's output: the young man is represented at the most dramatic moment, when all his strength is being put into the throw: his face is tense, his look concentrated on a precise point, while his curved body seems to pull back;
the result is that the figure breaks out of the limits of the block of stone from which it has been carved, far removed from the traditional immobility of XVI century sculpture; this becomes evident when one compares it to other sculptures of David executed in earlier times (from Donatello to Michelangelo).
Similarly, the figures comprising the next groups, the *Rape of Proserpine* and *Apollo and Daphne* [9, 10, 12, 13, 14, 15] seem to be in movement.

Jupiter and the goat Amalthea, 1615 marble group Rome, Galleria Borghese

The bust of *Paul V* [20], a still early work, and the *Cardinal Scipione Borghese* [21], two copies of which were carried out later, are useful in tracing the development of the Bernini portrait.
This moves from its initial static nature, evident in the calm attitude of absorption and simple drapery of the former, to the more dramatic effect of the latter, where a heightened vivacity gives us the illusion of being able to actually talk to the person represented.
The *bozzetto* for the *Equestriam monument of Louis XIV* [23] provides an insight into his ideas for equestrian monuments; in *Truth* [22] on the other hand, a new kind of "Rubensian" beauty can be observed, but it is above all the *Young self-portrait* [16] and its successor which allow us to appreciate the changes in his painting, classically inspired initially, then more dynamic, à la Velazquez (at which point one might mention another *Self-portrait* [40], now in Florence at the Uffizi).

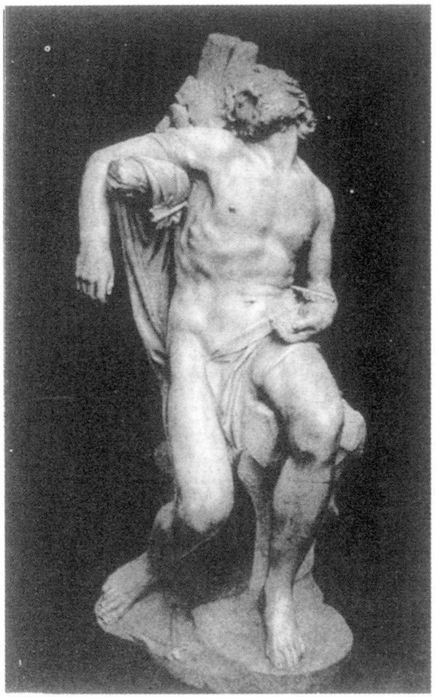

St. Sebastian, 1617-1618 ca., marble Lugano, Thyssen-Bornemisza Collection

The Vatican city

A series of great *oeuvres* by Bernini are to be found in the Vatican. The first of these is the *Baldacchino of St. Peter* [65], the project for which was started in 1624, and the last, the *Altar of the Sacrament* [75], terminated in 1673-74. These were highly demanding works which kept the sculptor occupied for years and, as a result of the long timespan involved, their characteristics tend to be very clearly defined.
After the Baldacchino came the *Tomb of Urban VIII* [66] which while following the model established by Giacomo della Porta with the tomb of Paul III, shows a greater chromatic balance.
Also noteworthy, in their surprisingly human attitudes, are the two figures of the virtues (Charity and Justice) situated either side of the monument.
Next in chronological order is the *St. Longinus* [67] where the drapery is given the express function of accentuating the dramatic force of the subject: three rounds of folds which originate from a sort of knot below the left arm open out into a rich display of material, leading the eye towards the lance, a relic of which is conserved in the crypt below.
The *Tomb of Countess Matilde* [64] and the almost contemporary relief *Pasce Oves Meas* [73], placed on the interior of the portico above the central door of the basilica, show a less Baroque, more Classical tendency, to which the statue of *Urban VIII* [37] in the Palazzo dei Conservatori (1635-1640) also belongs. The *Cathedra of St. Peter* [71, 72], the most "Baroque" of Bernini's works, is situated in the apse of the basilica. It is a large sculptural-architectonic group executed in different materials including bronze, stucco and marble, conceived as a grandiose vision bathed in the golden light that flows through the window placed at the centre of the group of angels. Its effect becomes even more dramatic when seen from the central nave through the great baldacchino which serves to frame it.
In the portico of the basilica, beside the door leading to the *Scala Regia* [76], another important work by Bernini, one can admire the *Equestrian Monument to Constantine* [70], theatrical, but innovatory when compared to other equestrian statues.
The *Colonnade* [68, 69, 74] of Piazza San Pietro present Bernini with the task of finding a solution to the problem of delimiting the piazza. He does this spectacularly, by building two wings which branch off from the facade of the basilica, converging slightly at the beginning, to then open out into a semi-circular colonnade. Here, Bernini symbolically represents the church of Peter, and its ability to embrace the whole of the Christian world. An effect of surprise and wonder must have been felt by the visitor, arriving from the narrow streets of the Borgo, on suddenly seeing before him the great complex of the square; an effect somewhat diminished by the construction of the large via della Conciliazione during the Fascist period.

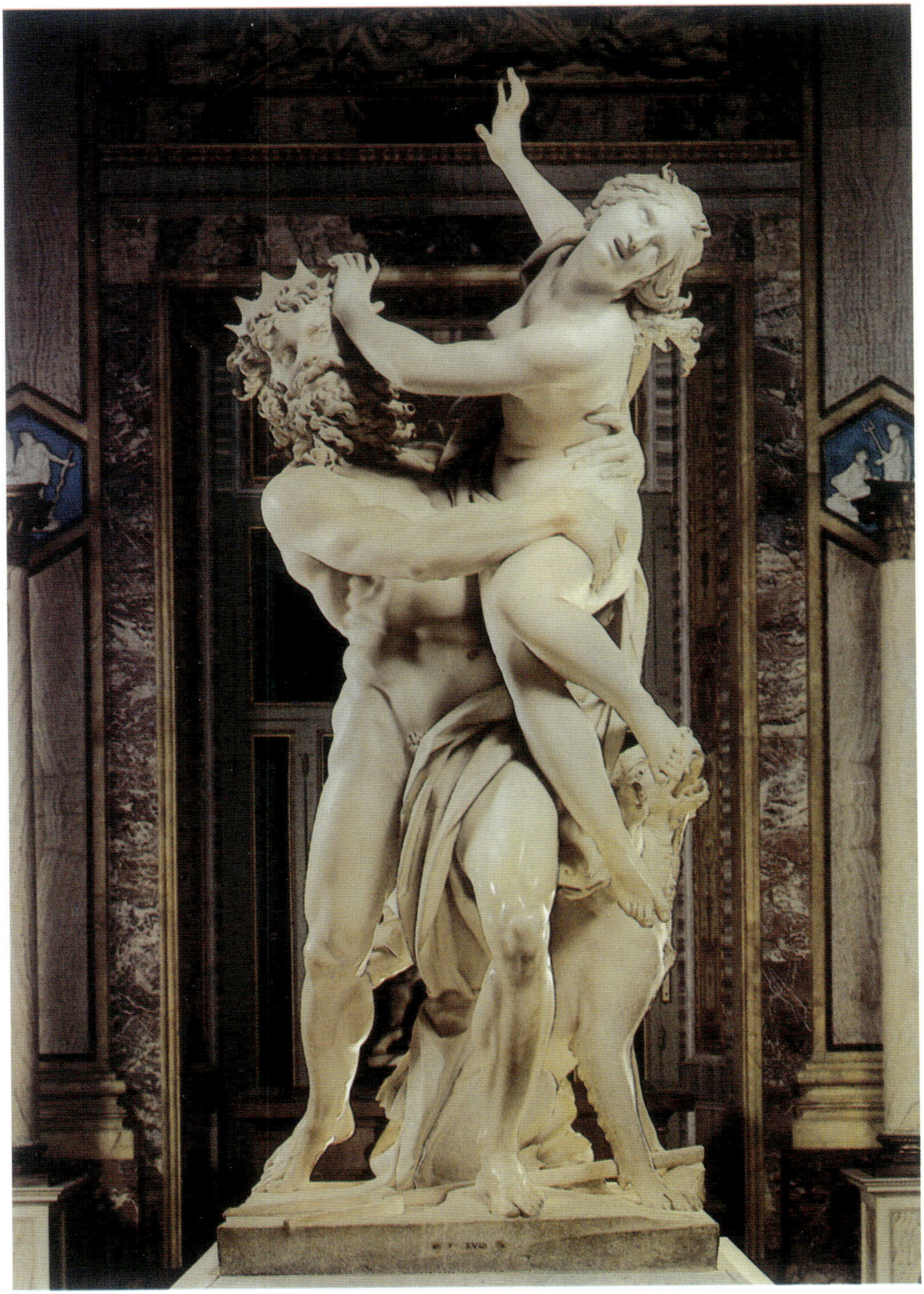

The rape of Proserpine (1612-1622), marble group. Rome, Galleria Borghese

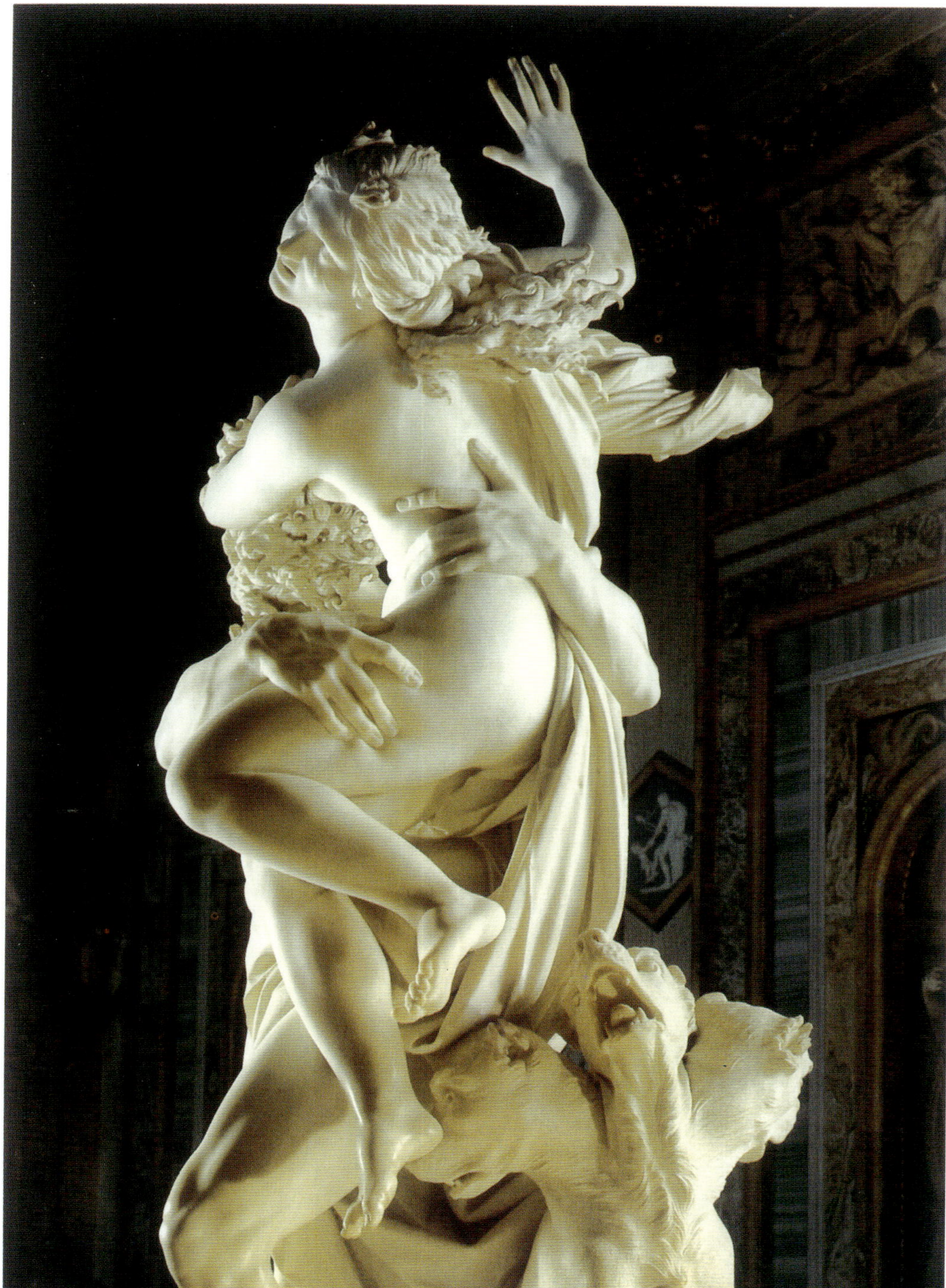

The rape of Proserpine, detail (1612-1622), marble group. Rome, Galleria Borghese

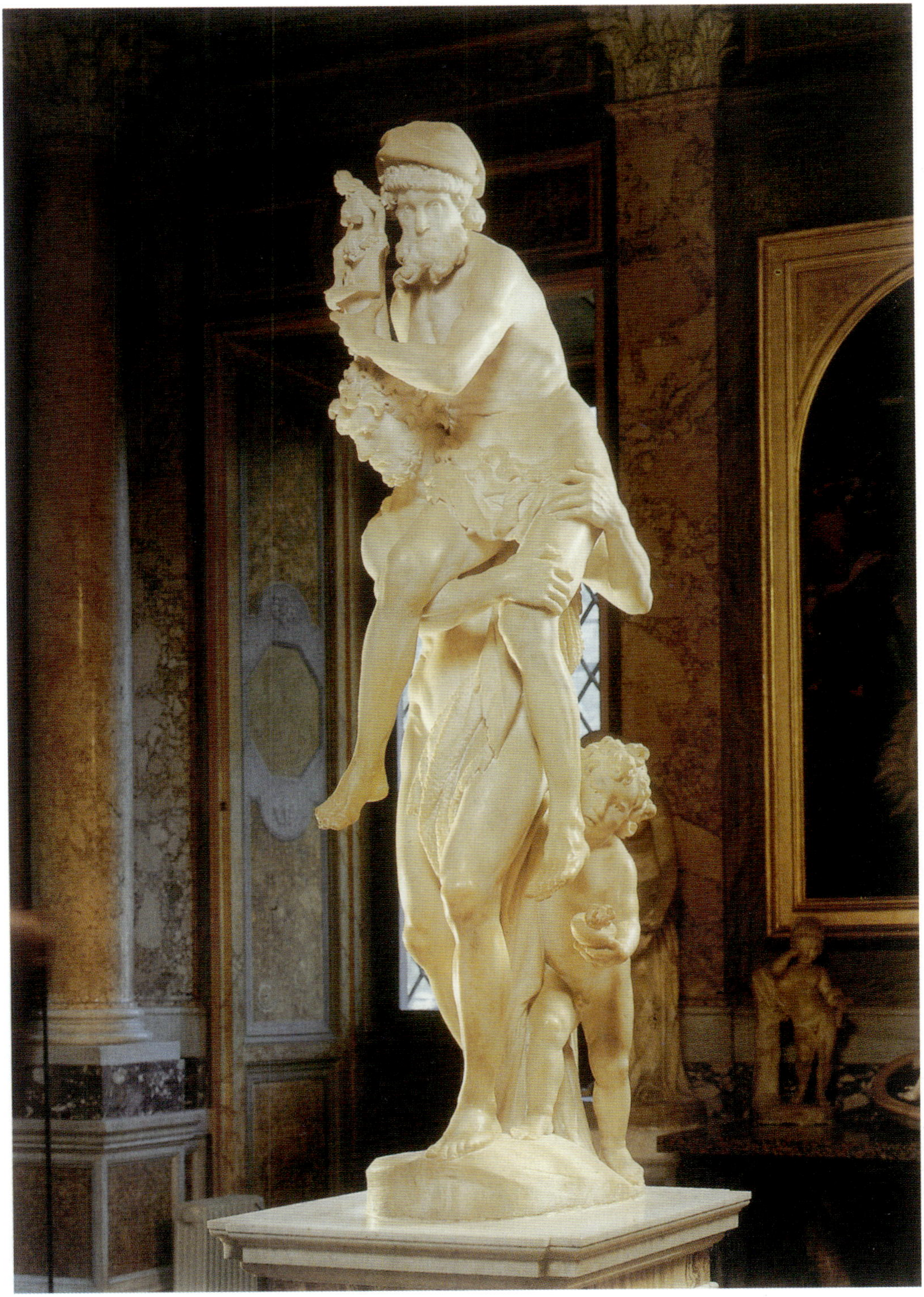

Aeneas, Anchises and Ascanius (1618-1619), marble group. Rome, Galleria Borghese

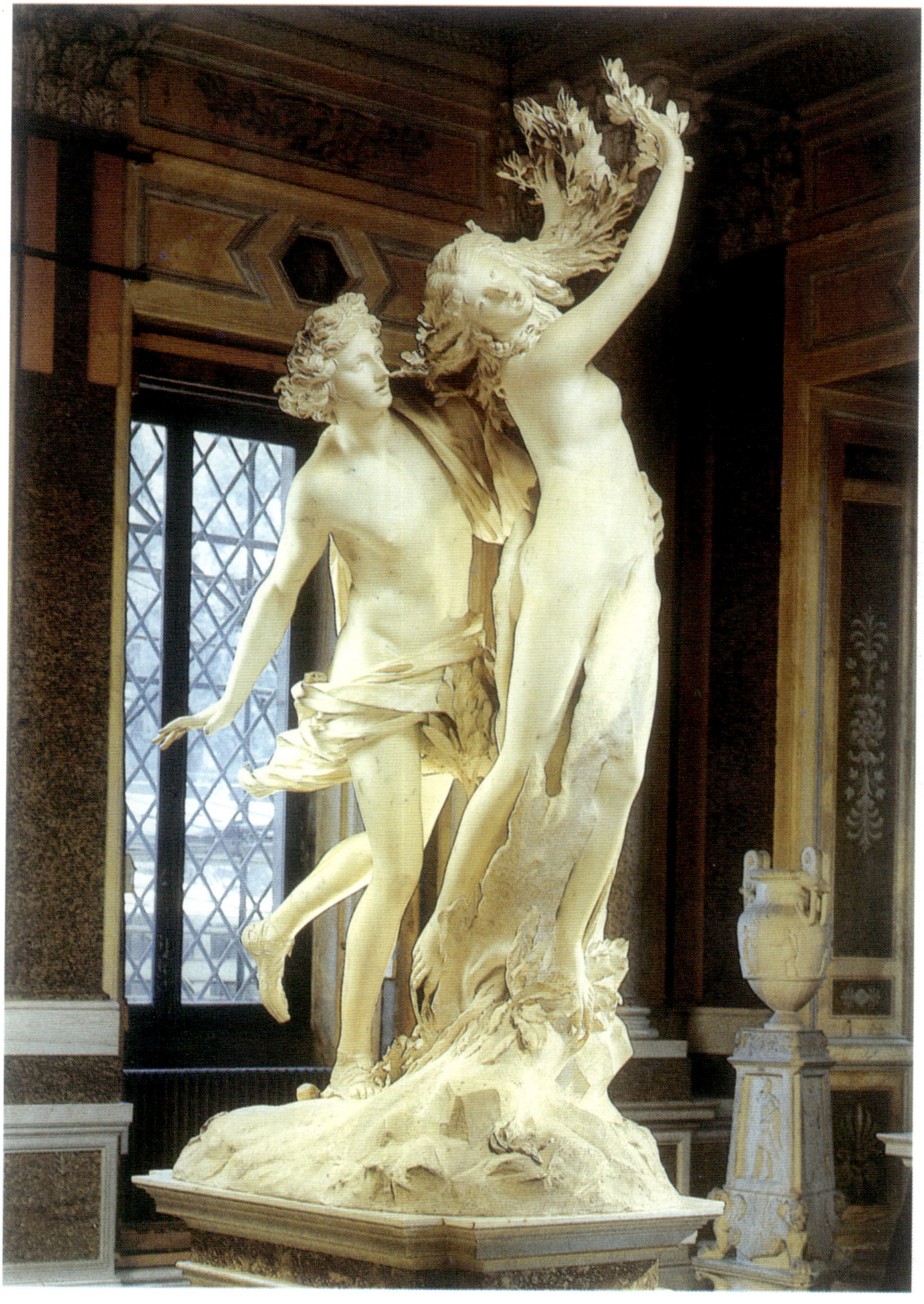

Apollo and Daphne (1622-1624), marble group. Rome, Galleria Borghese

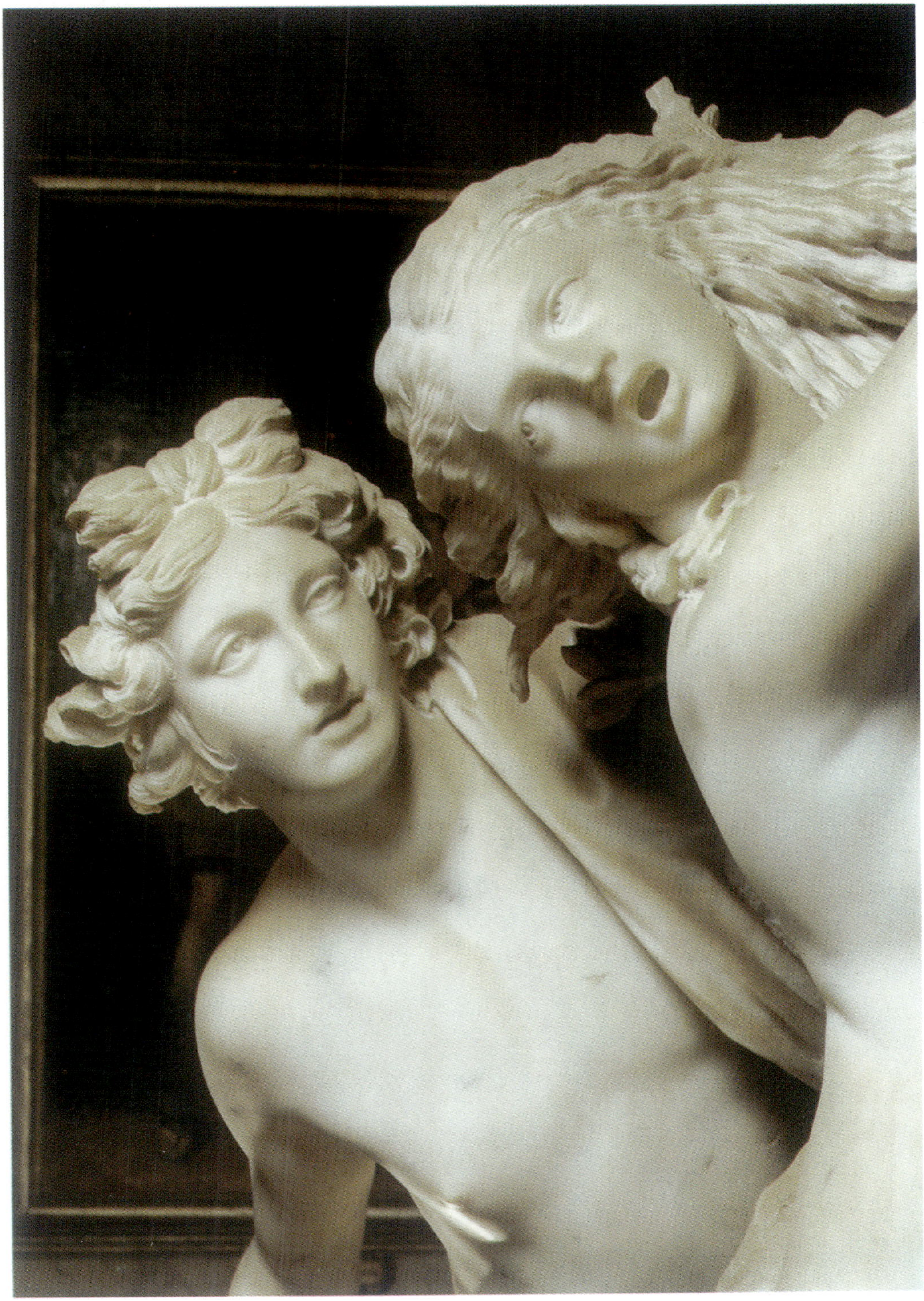

Apollo and Daphne, detail (1622-1624), marble group. Rome, Galleria Borghese

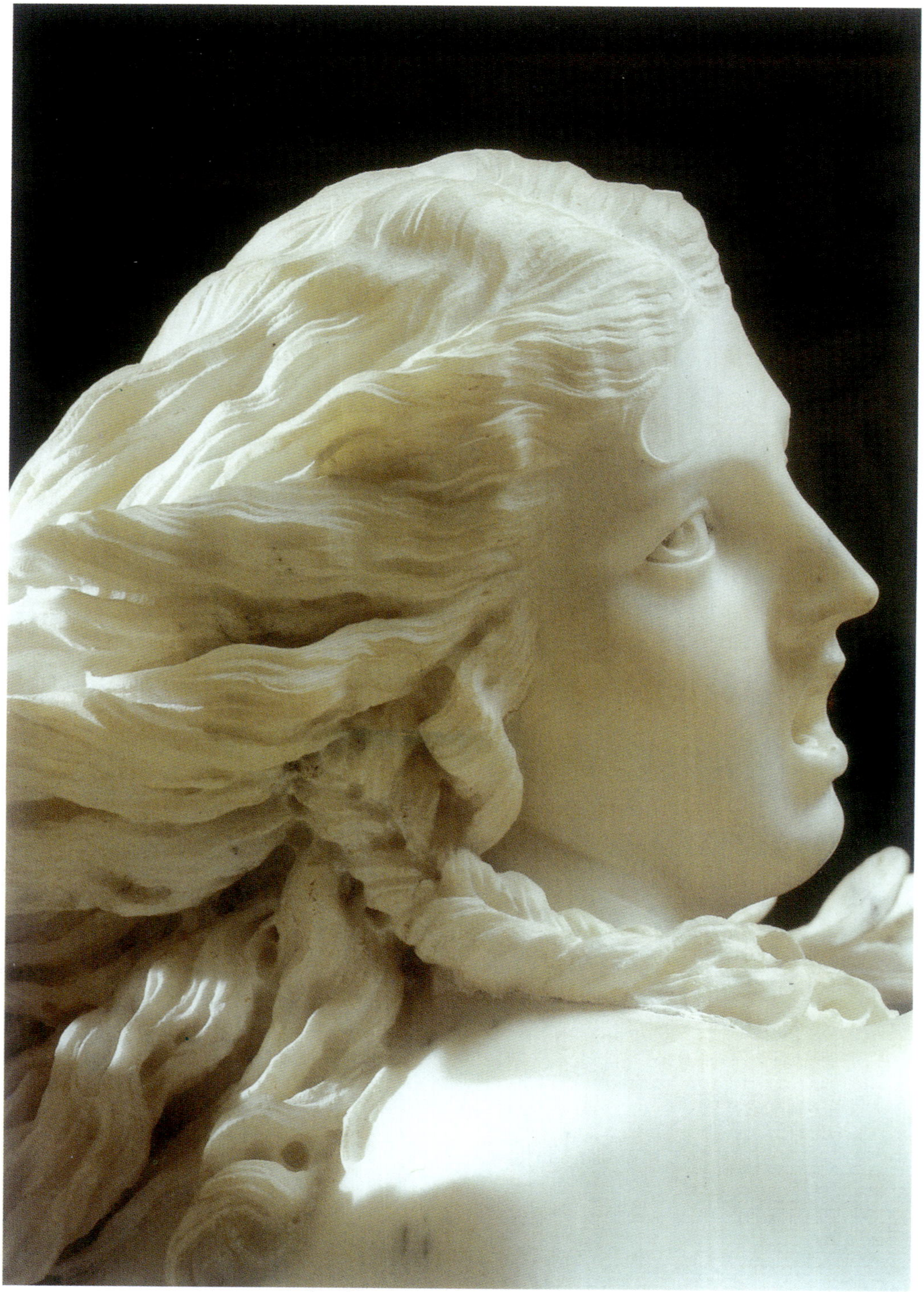

Apollo and Daphne, detail (1622-1624), marble group. Rome, Galleria Borghese

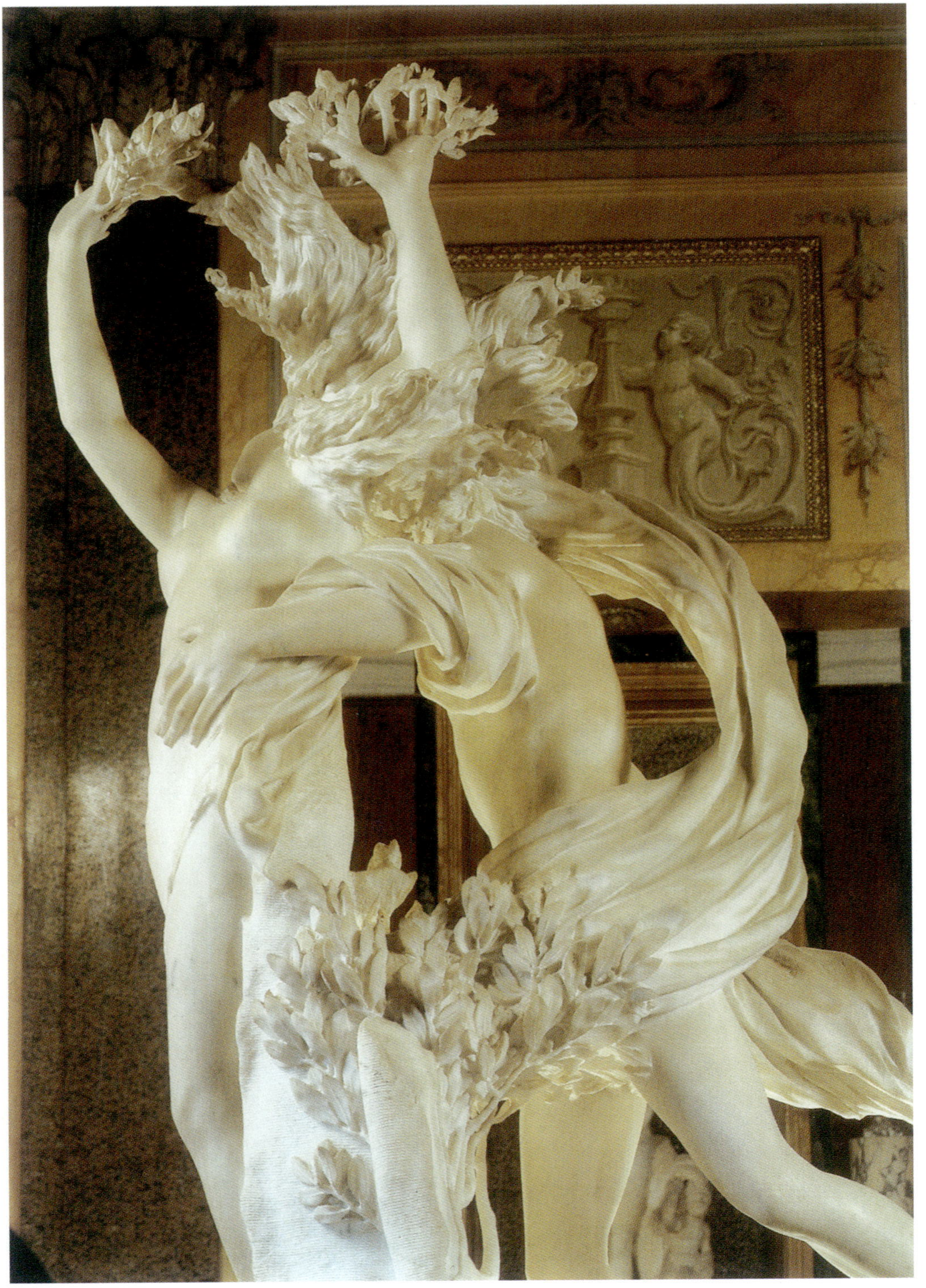

Apollo and Daphne, detail (1622-1624), marble group. Rome, Galleria Borghese

Young self-portrait (1623), oil on canvas, Rome, Galleria Borghese

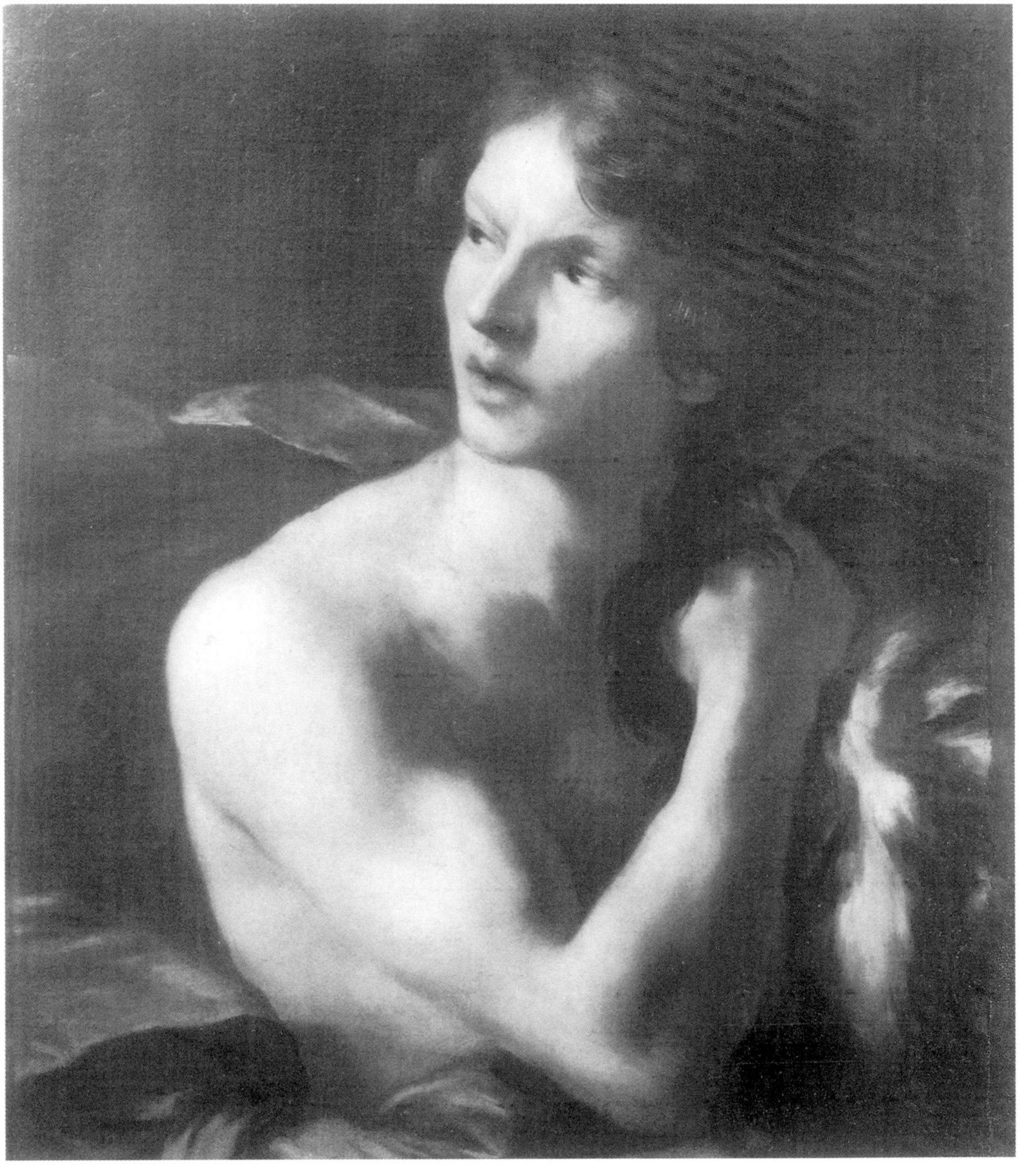

David (1623), oil on canvas, Rome, Palazzo Barberini

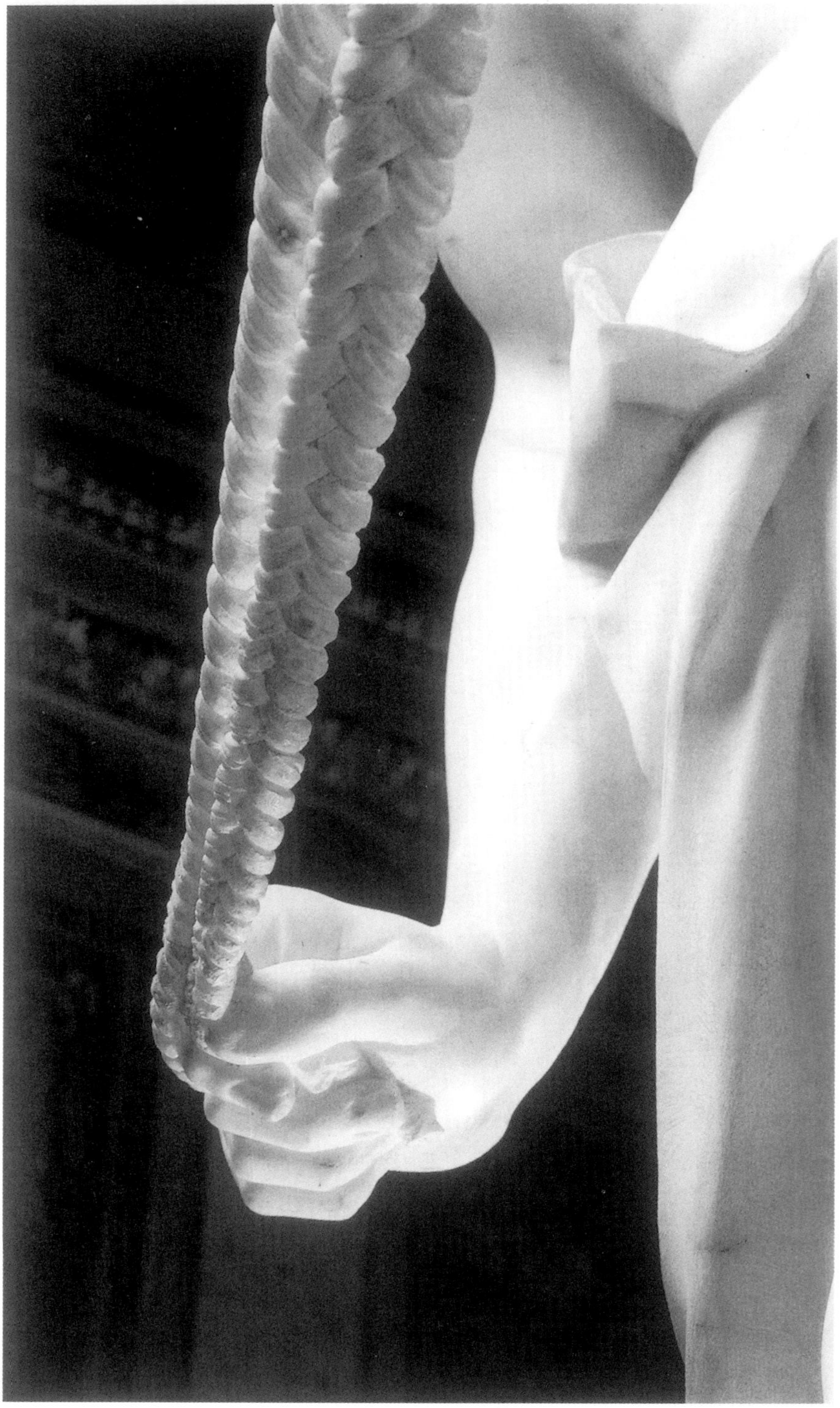

David, detail (1623), marble. Rome, Galleria Borghese

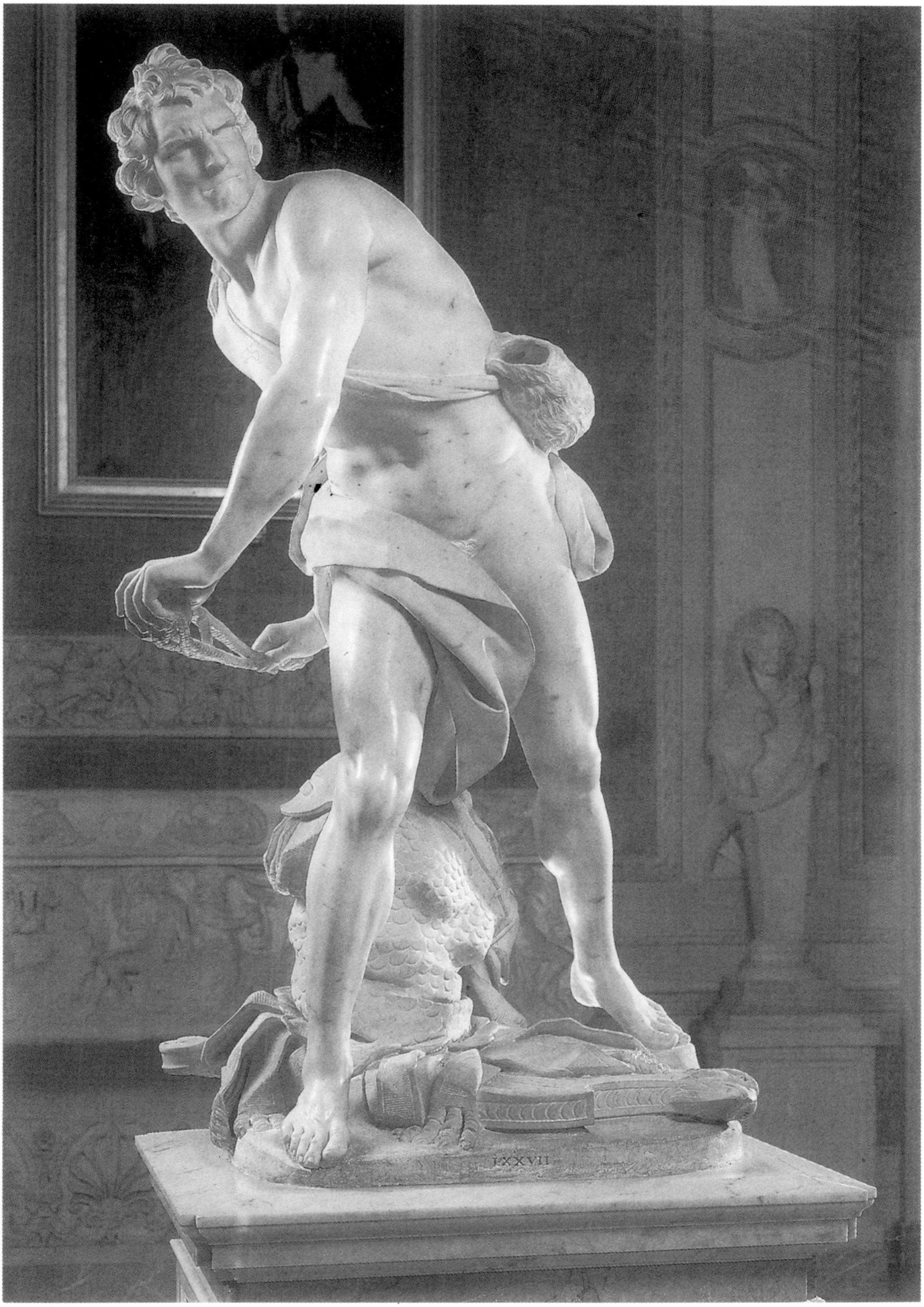

David (1623), marble. Rome, Galleria Borghese

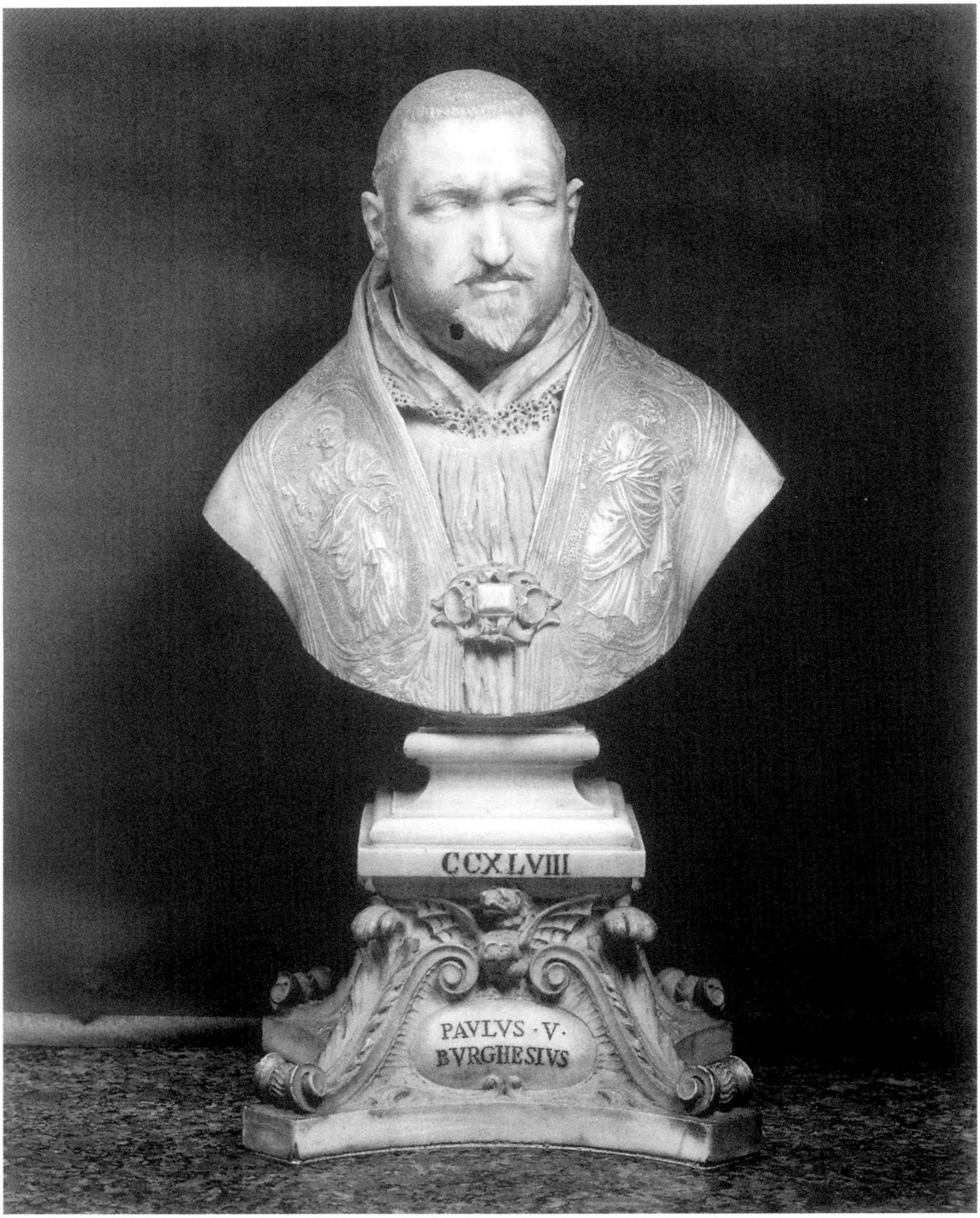

Paul V (1618), marble. Rome, Galleria Borghese

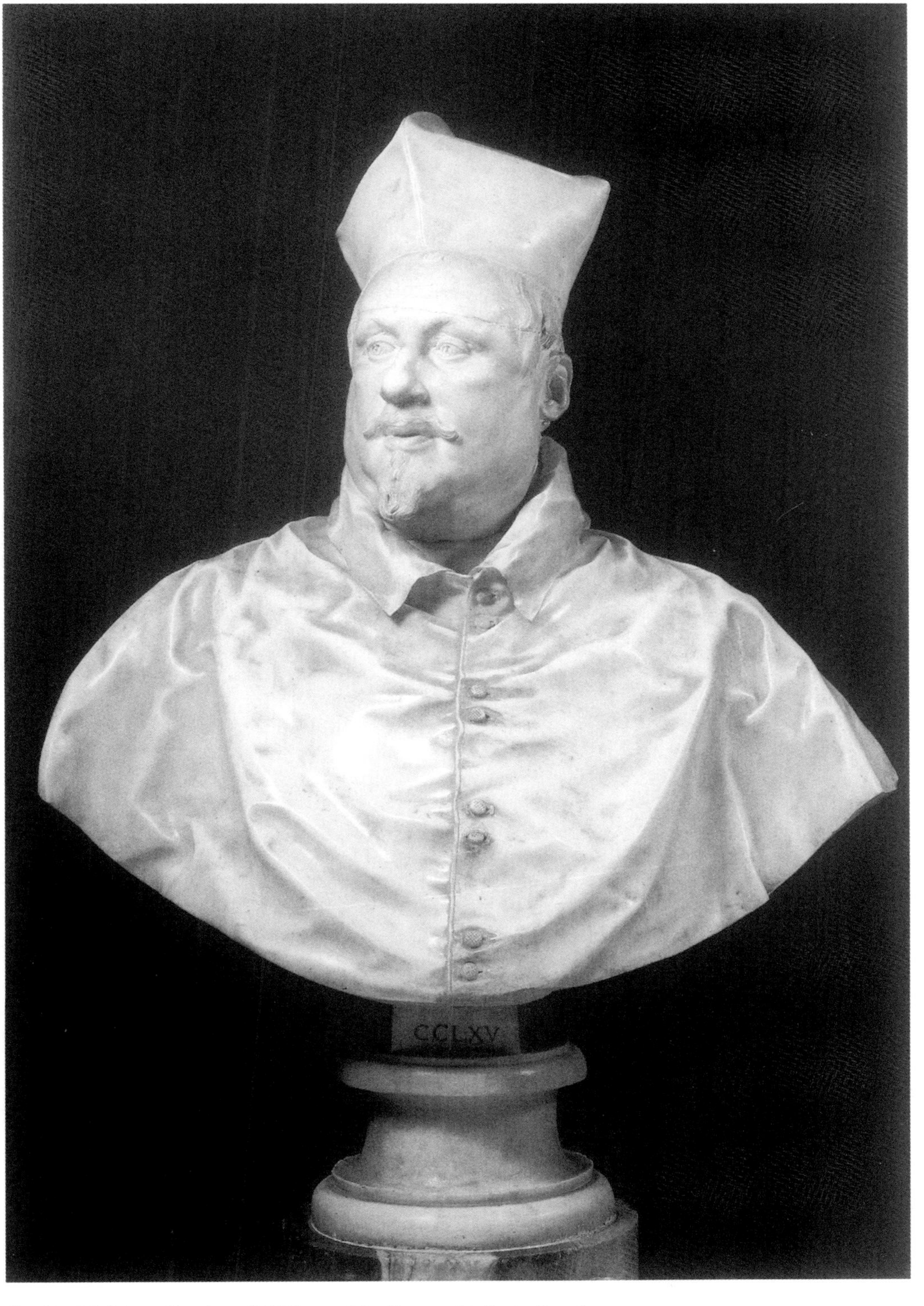

Cardinal Scipione Borghese (1632), marble. Rome, Galleria Borghese

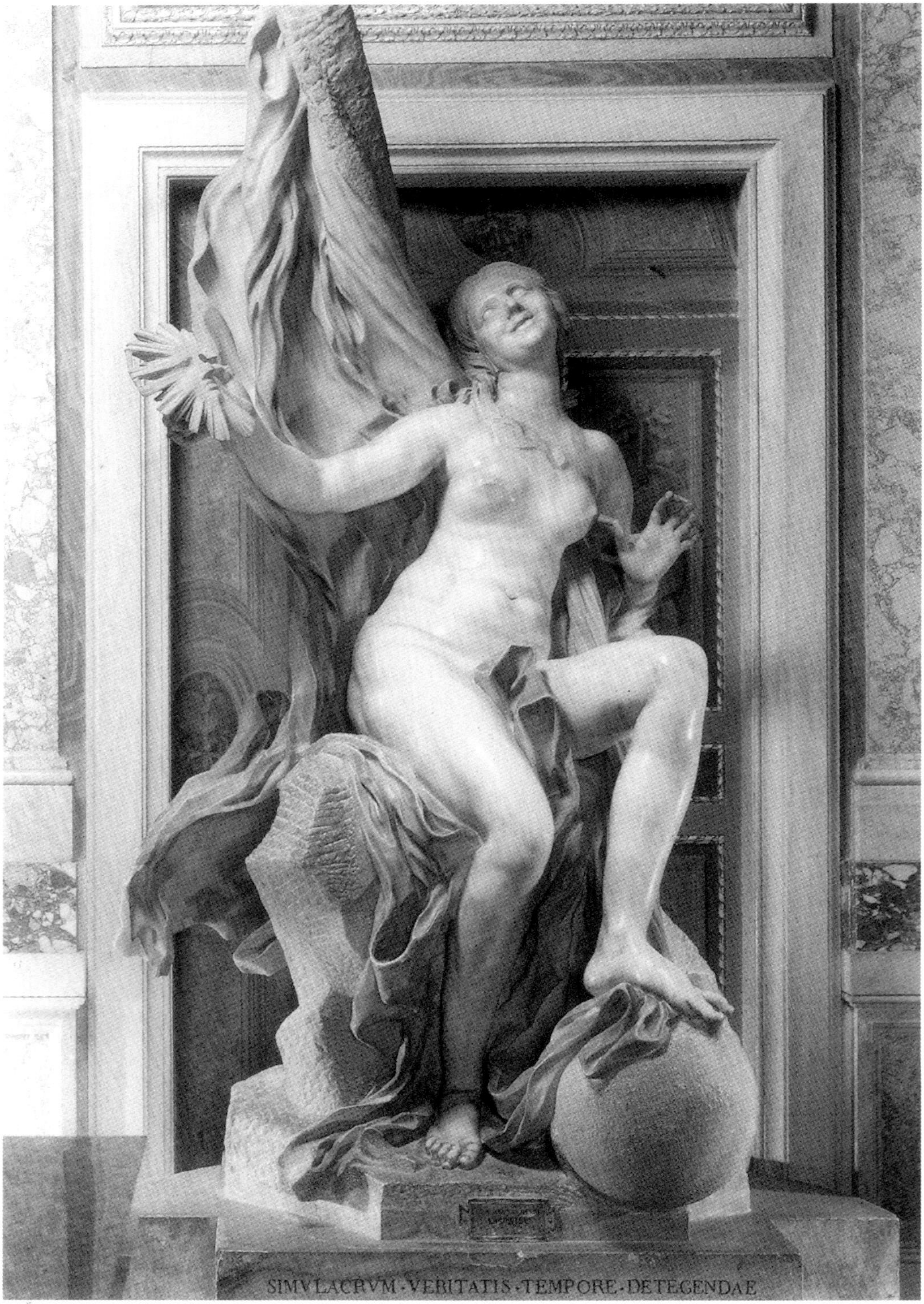

Truth (1646-1652), marble. Rome, Galleria Borghese

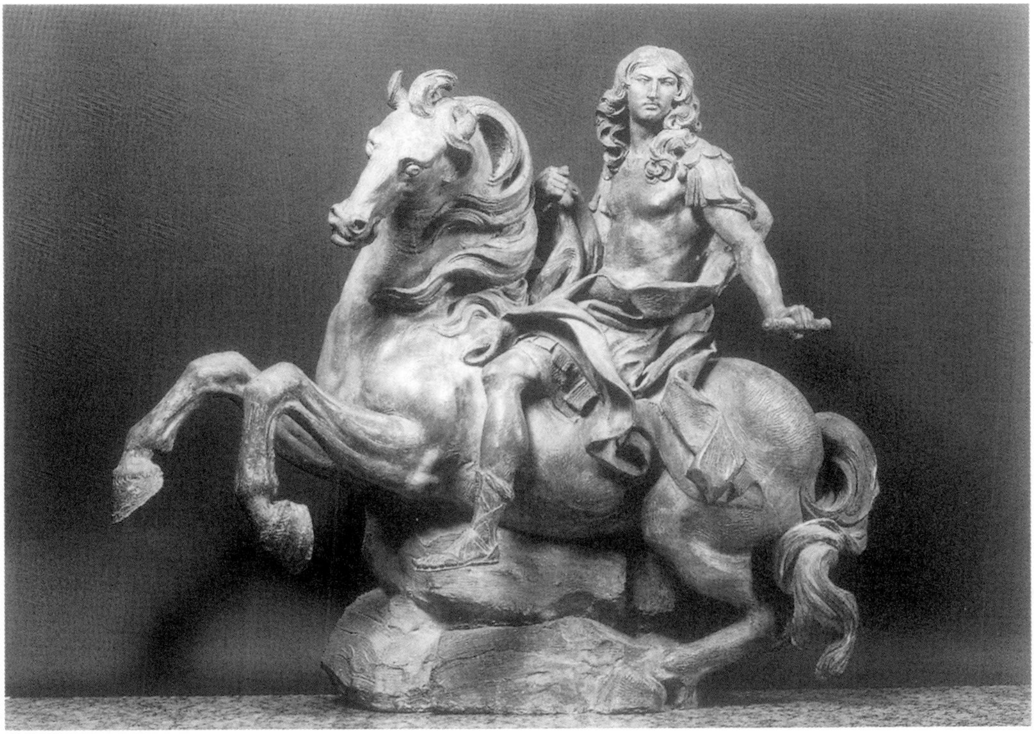

Bozzetto for monument to Louis XIV (1667 ca.), terracotta. Rome, Galleria Borghese

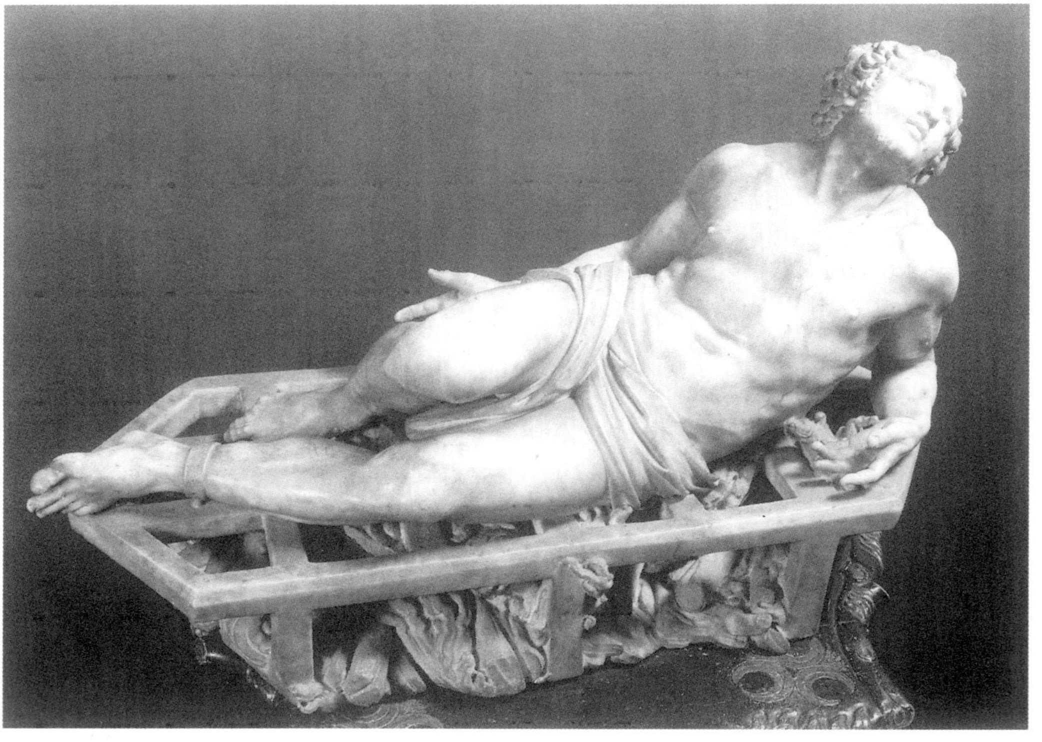

St. Laurence (1617 ca.), marble. Florence, Contini-Bonacossi Collection

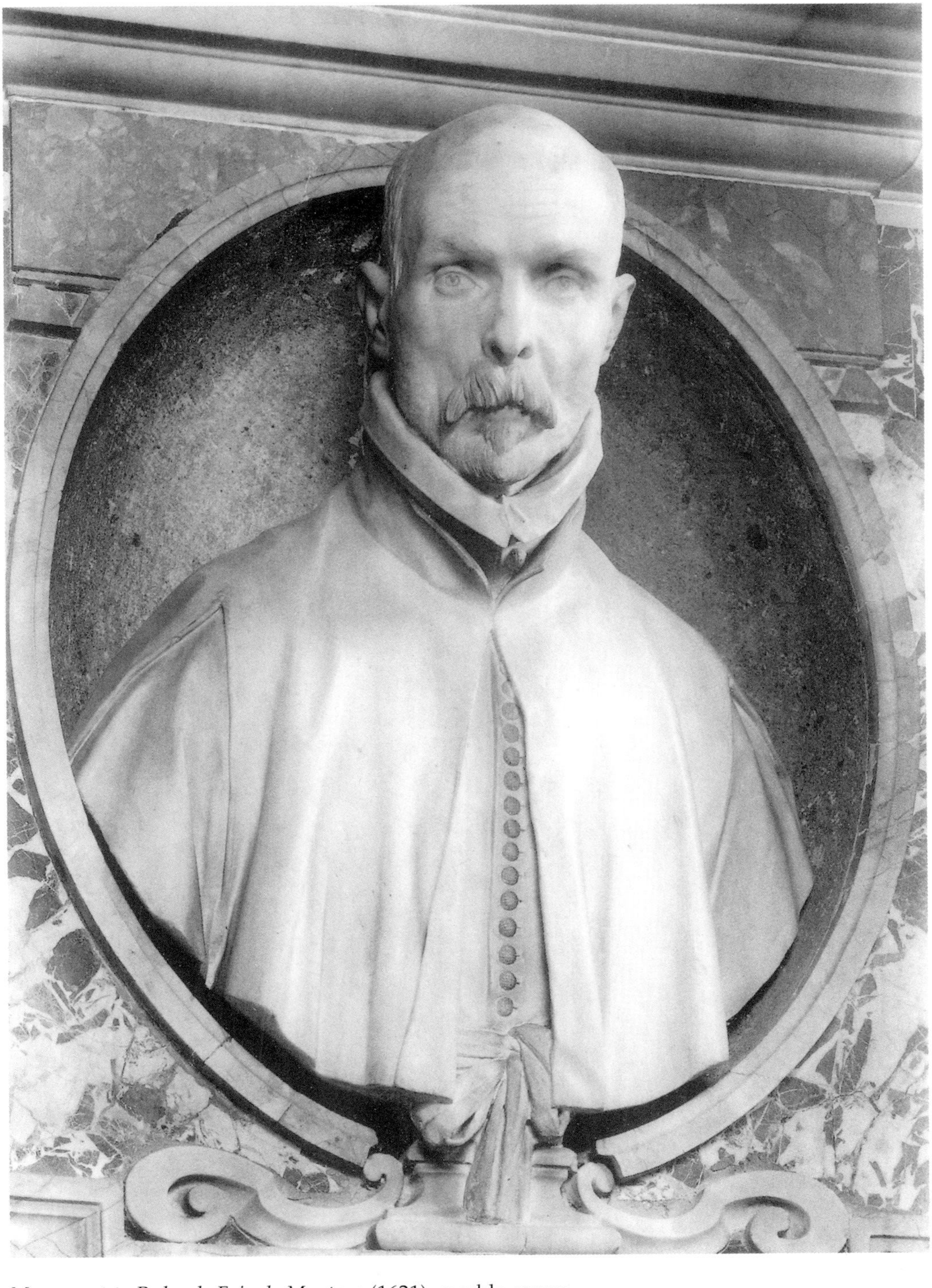

Monument to Pedro de Foix de Montoya (1621), marble group.
Rome, Church of Santa Maria di Monserrato

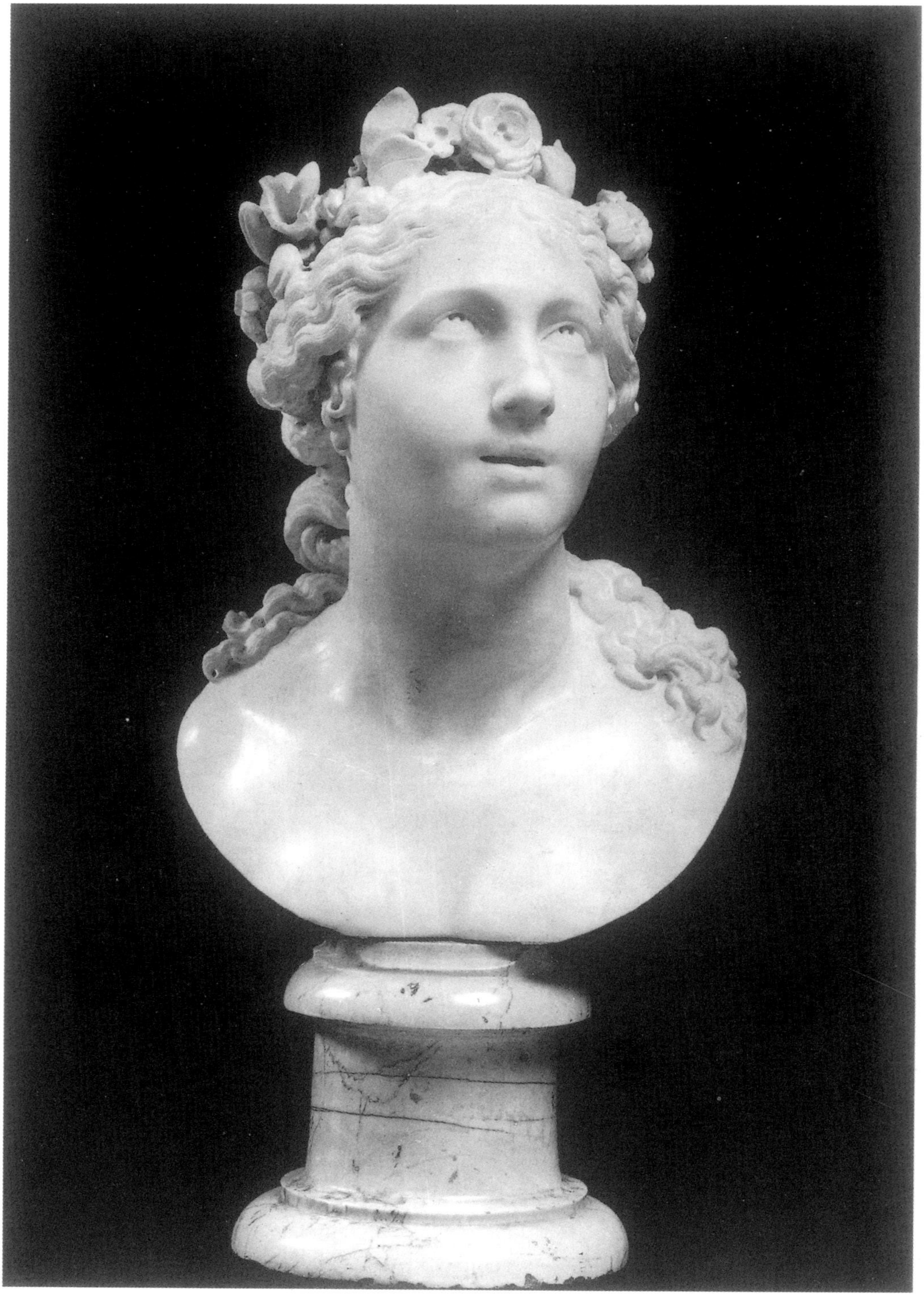

Anima Beata (1619), marble. Rome, Palazzo dell'Ambasciata di Spagna

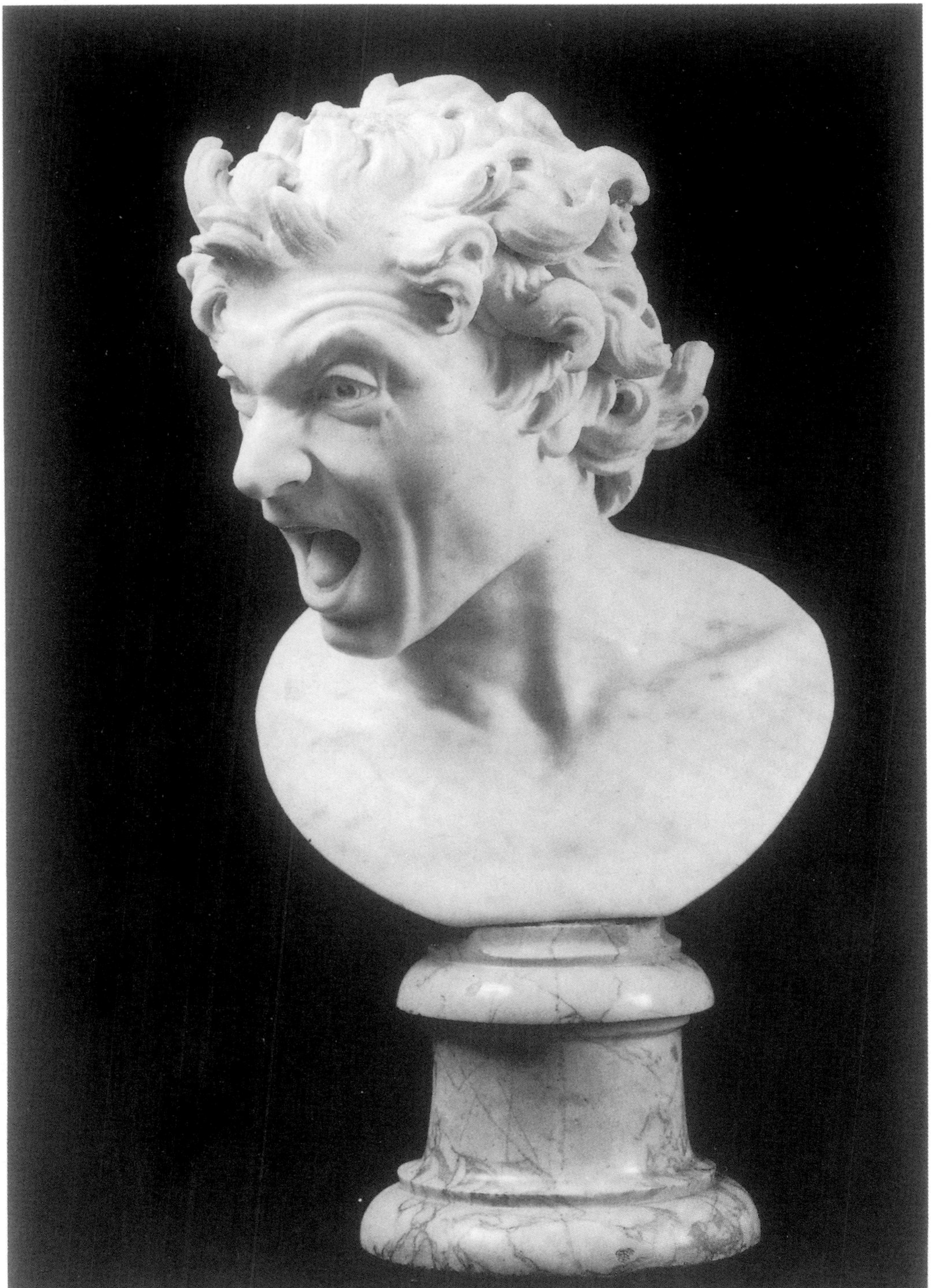

Anima Dannata (1619), marble. Rome, Palazzo dell'Ambasciata di Spagna

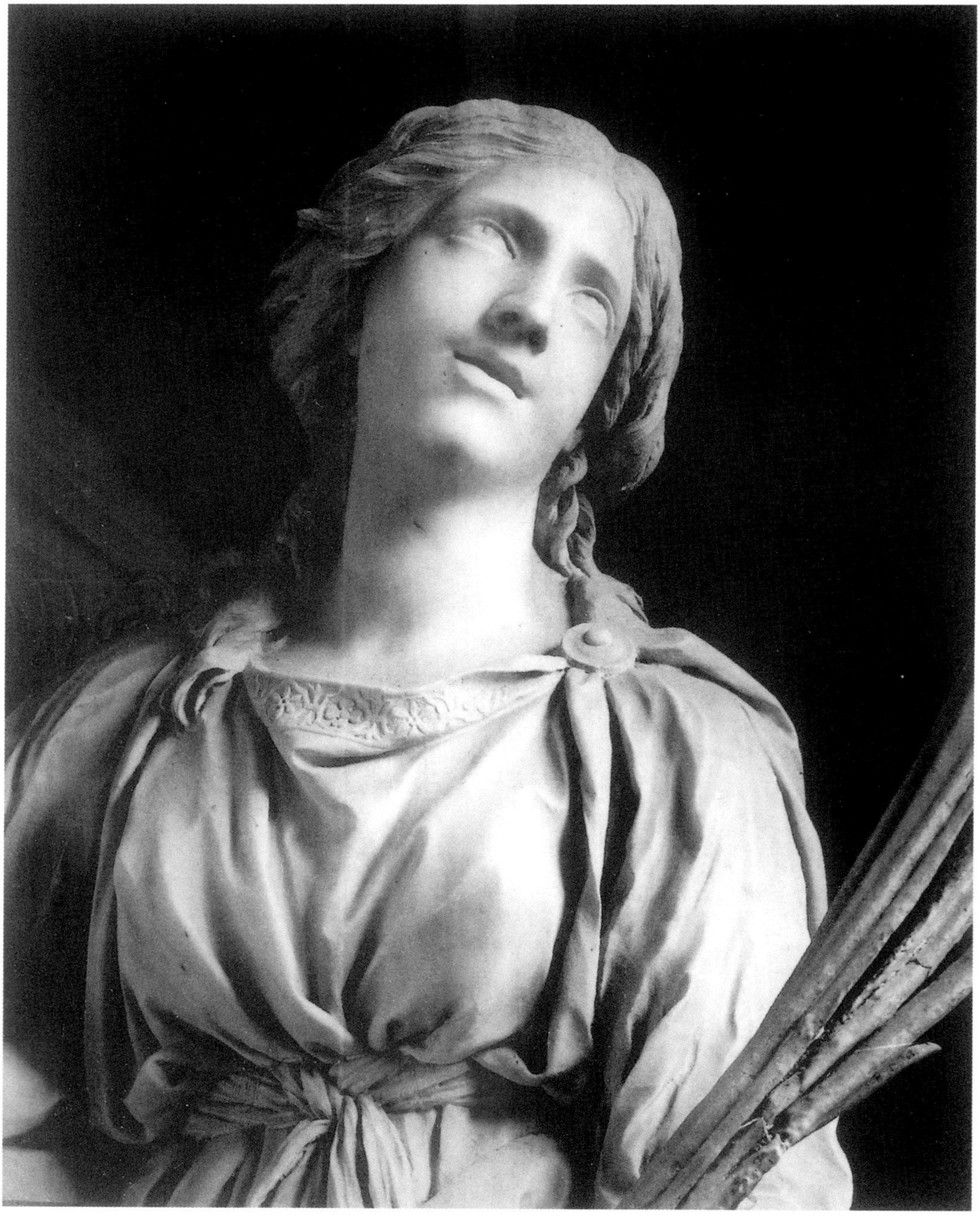

St. Bibiana (1624-1626), marble. Rome, Church of Santa Bibiana

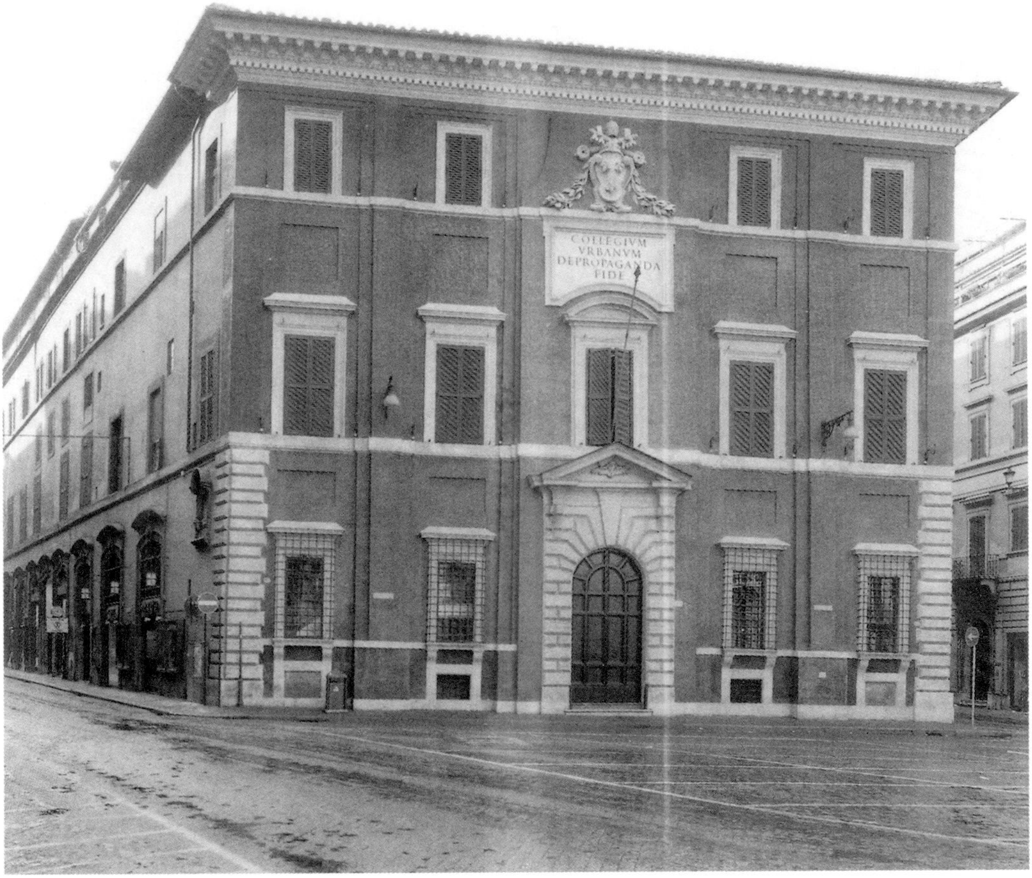

Facade (1627). Rome, Palazzo di Propaganda Fide

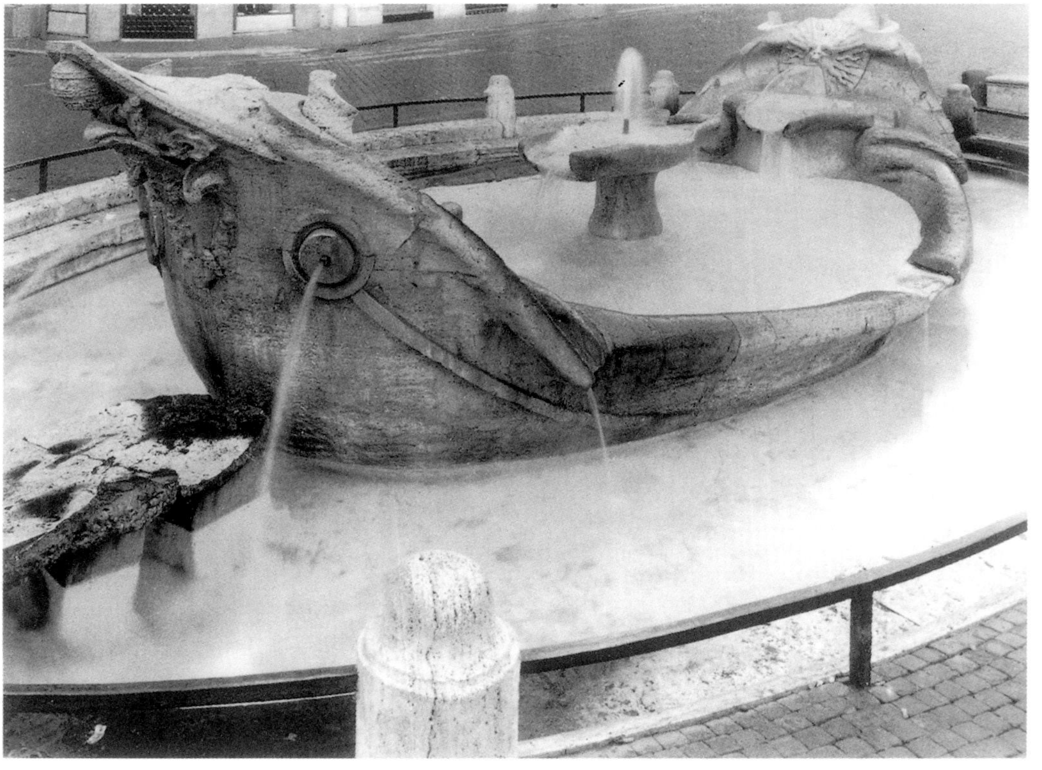

Fontana della Barcaccia (1627-1629), travertine stone. Rome, Piazza di Spagna

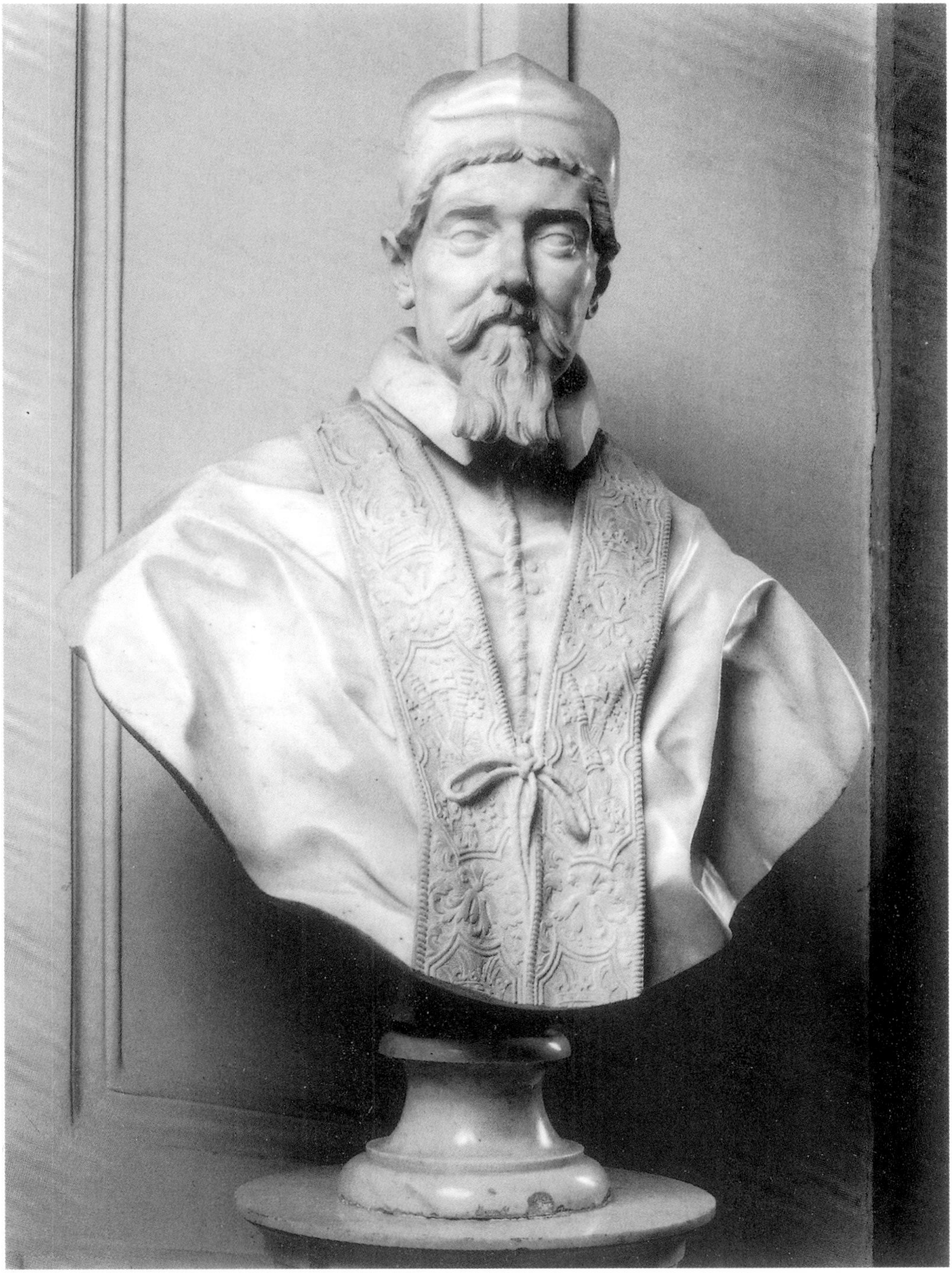

Urban VIII (1630), marble. Rome, Palazzo Barberini

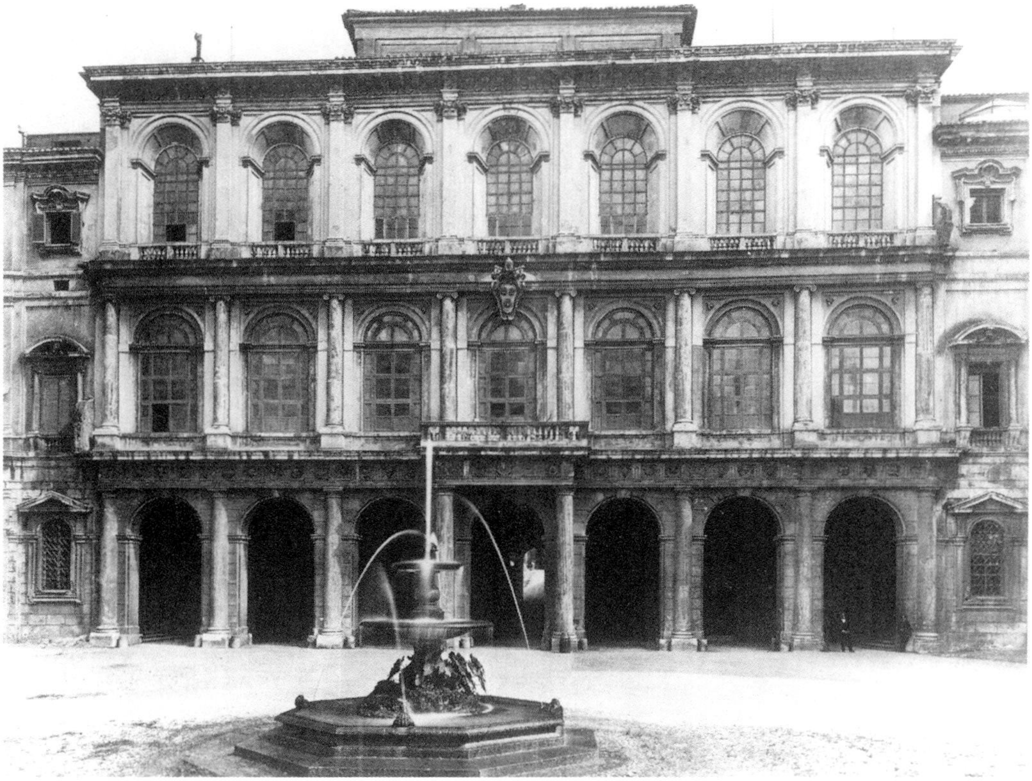

Facade (1627-1630). Rome, Palazzo Barberini

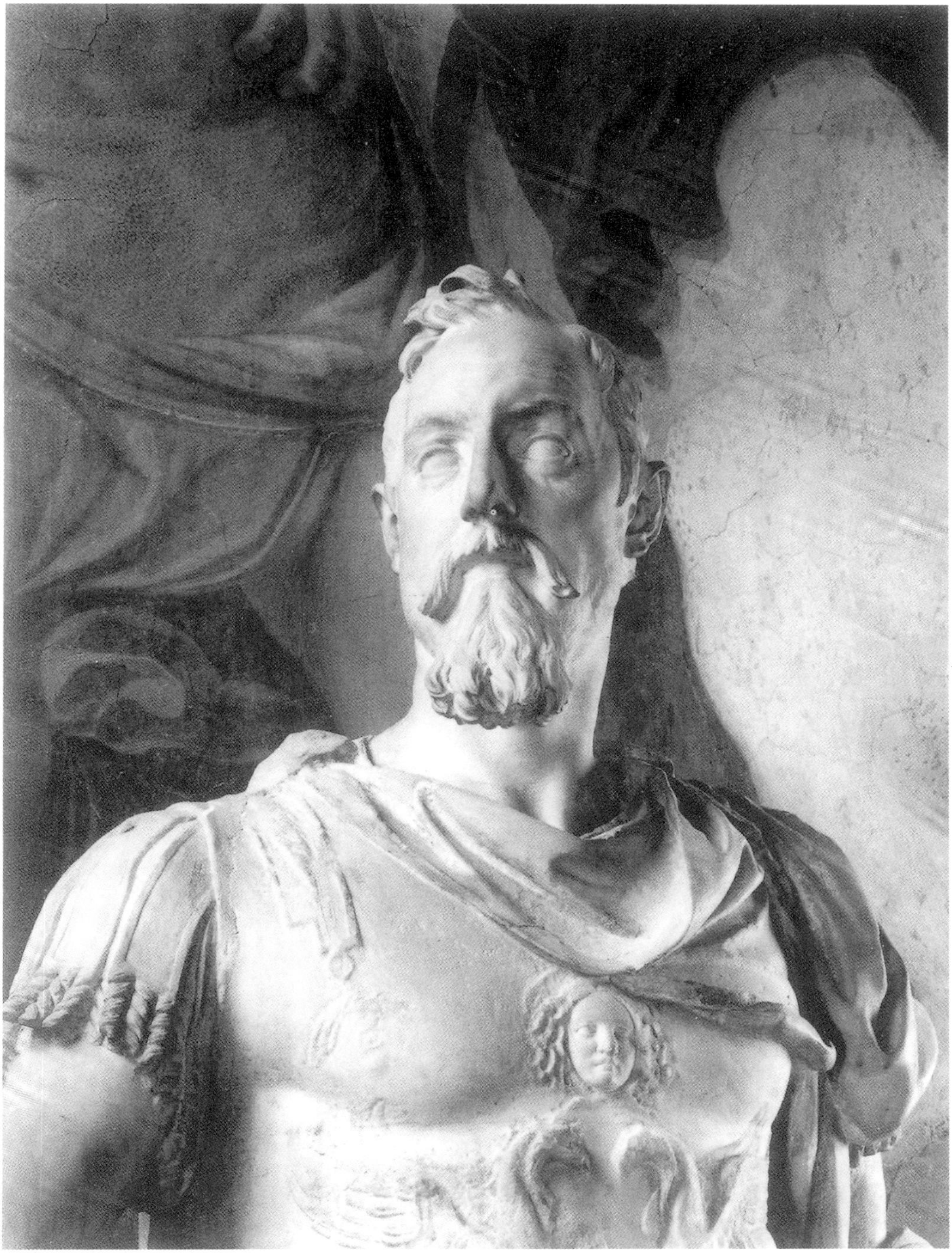

Carlo Barberini (1630), marble. Rome, Musei Capitolini

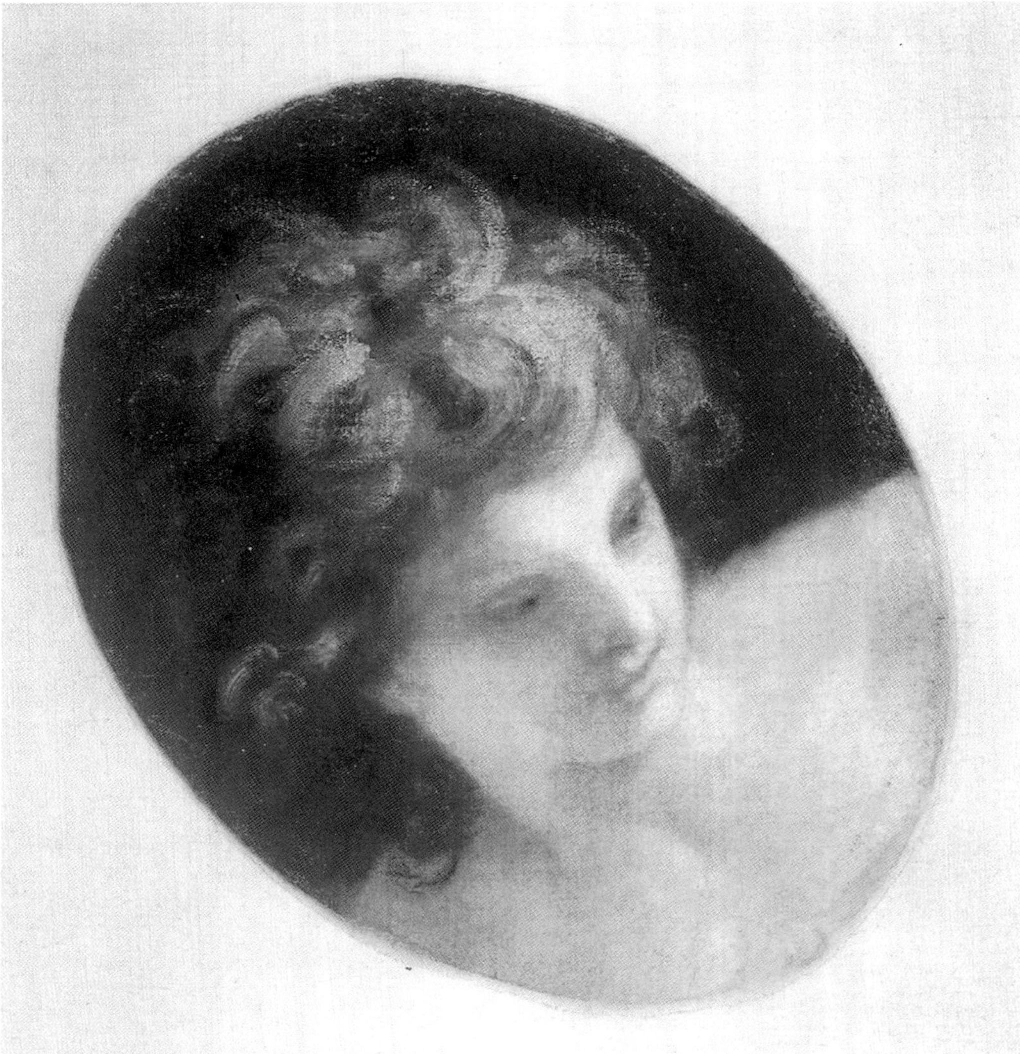

Head of an Angel (1630 ca.), oil on canvas. Florence, Uffizi

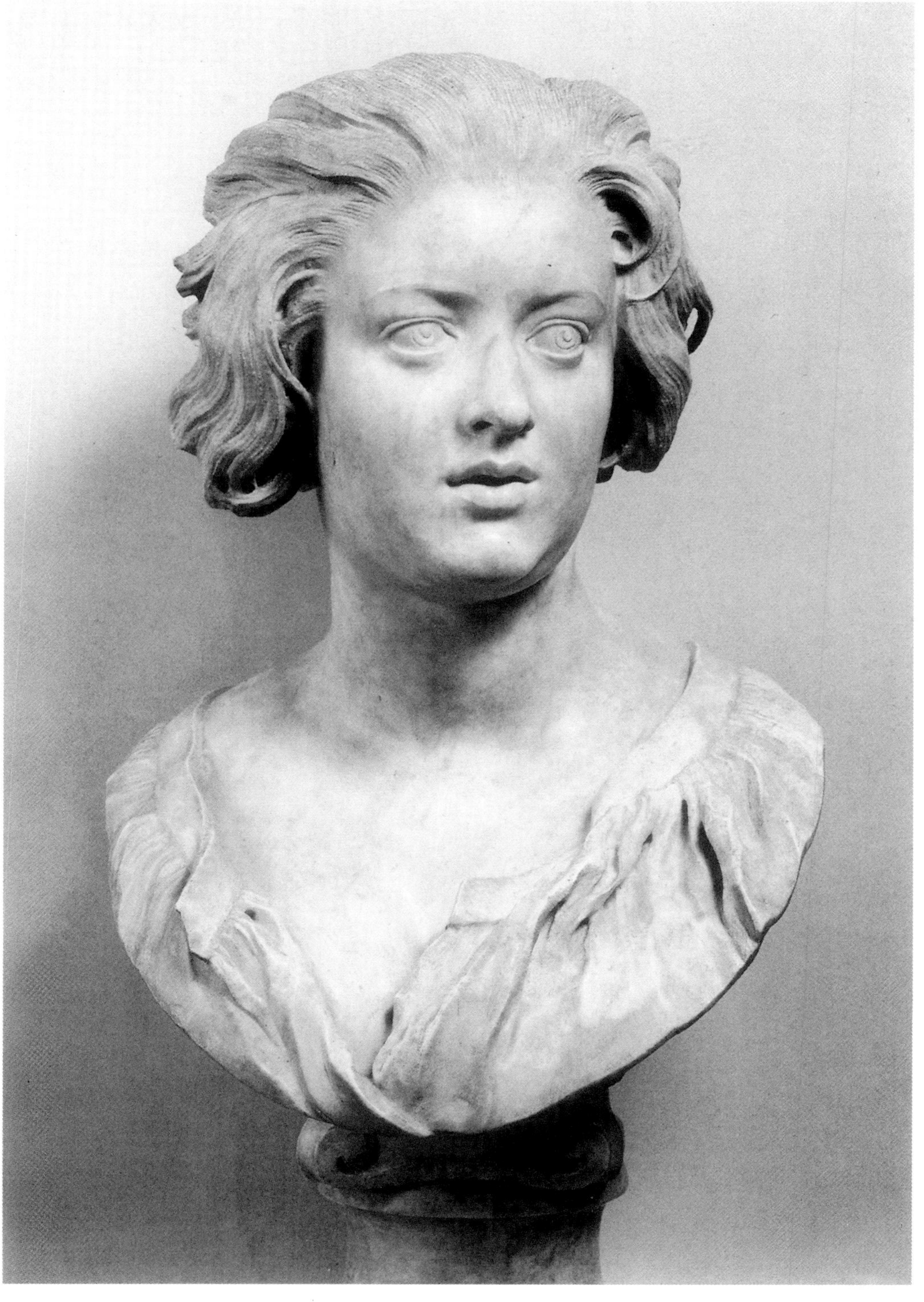

Costanza Bonarelli (1635), marble. Florence, Museo Nazionale del Bargello

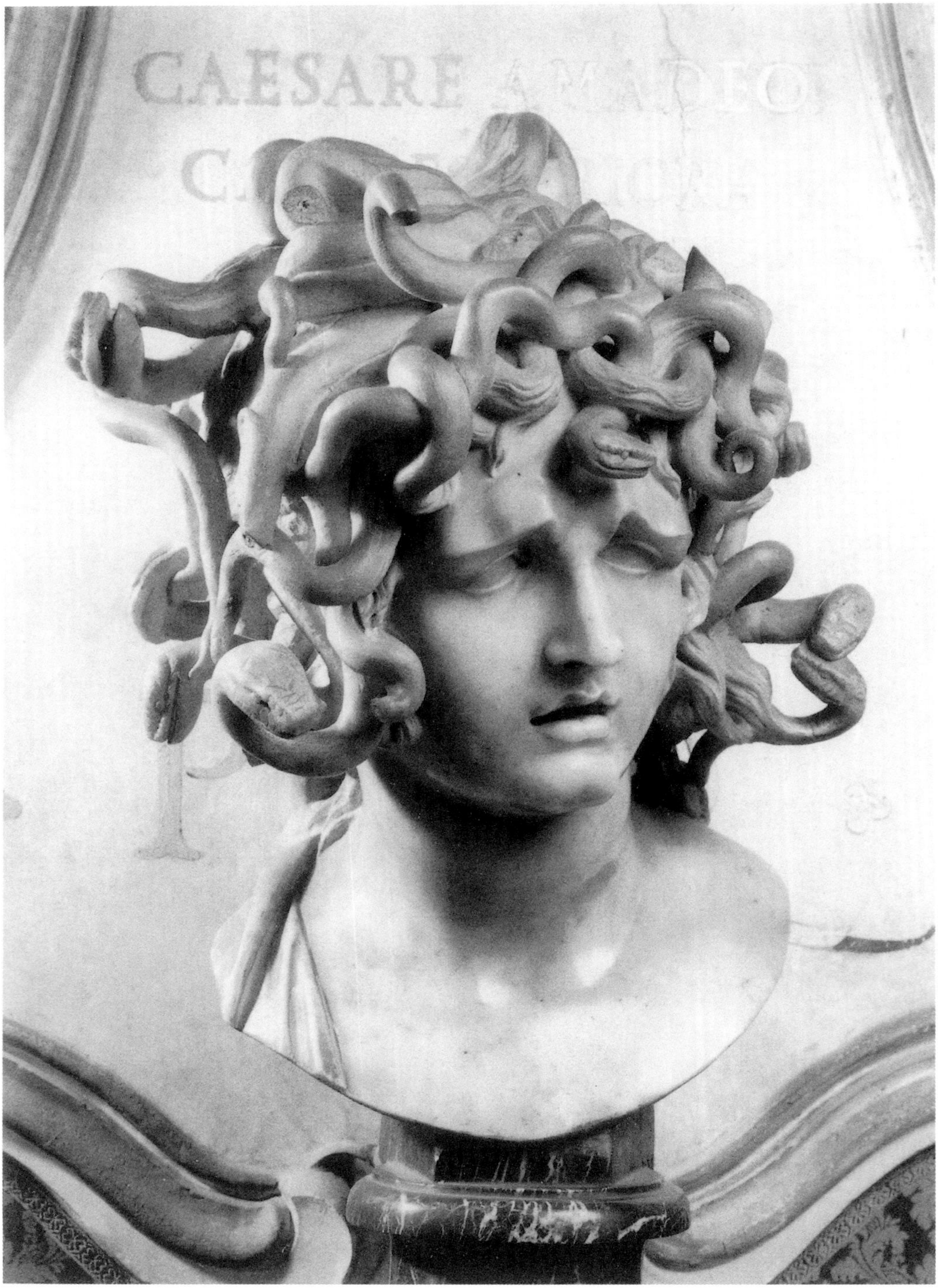

Medusa (1635 ca.), marble. Rome, Palazzo dei Conservatori

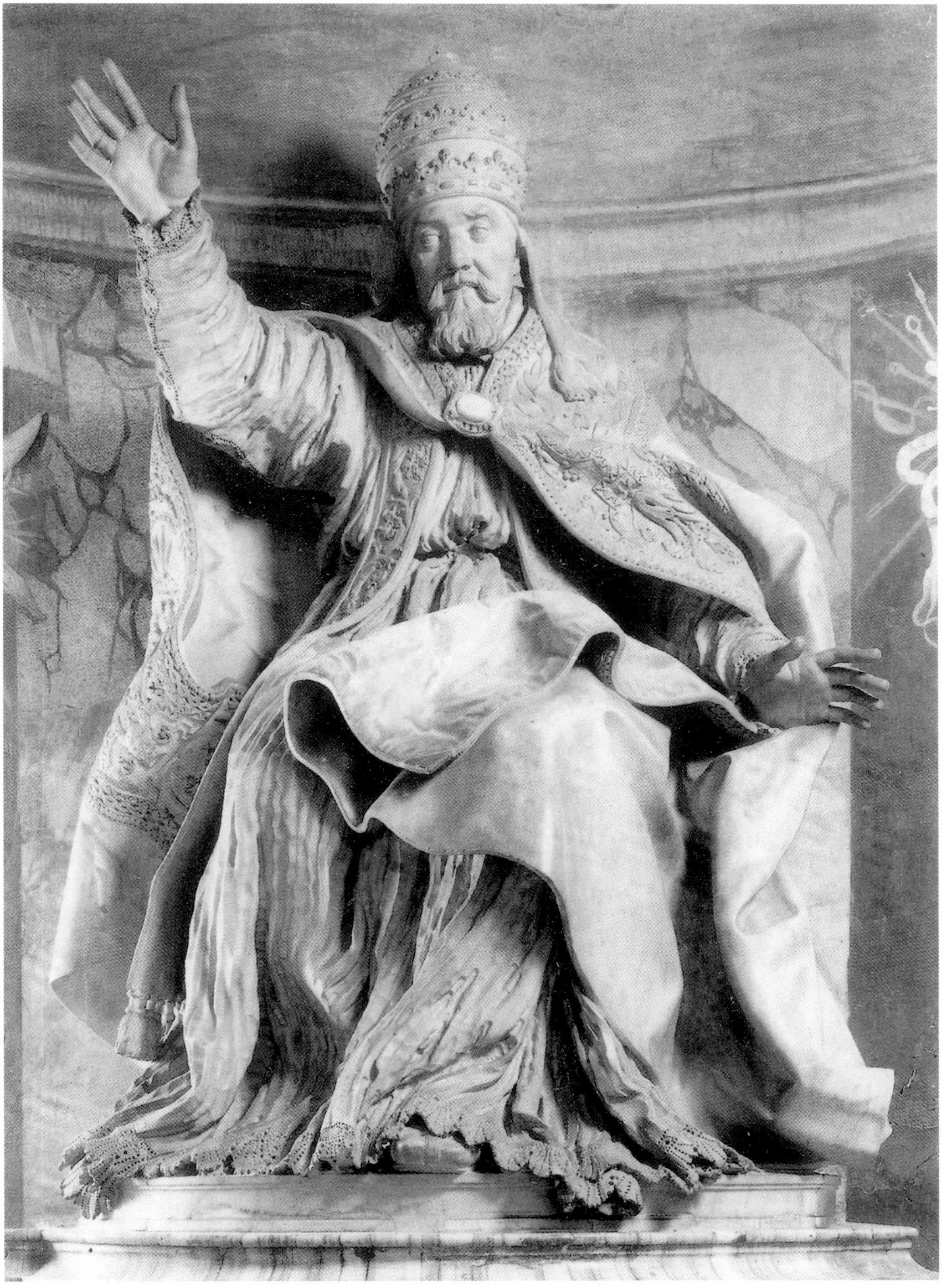

Urban VIII (1635-1640), marble. Rome, Palazzo dei Conservatori

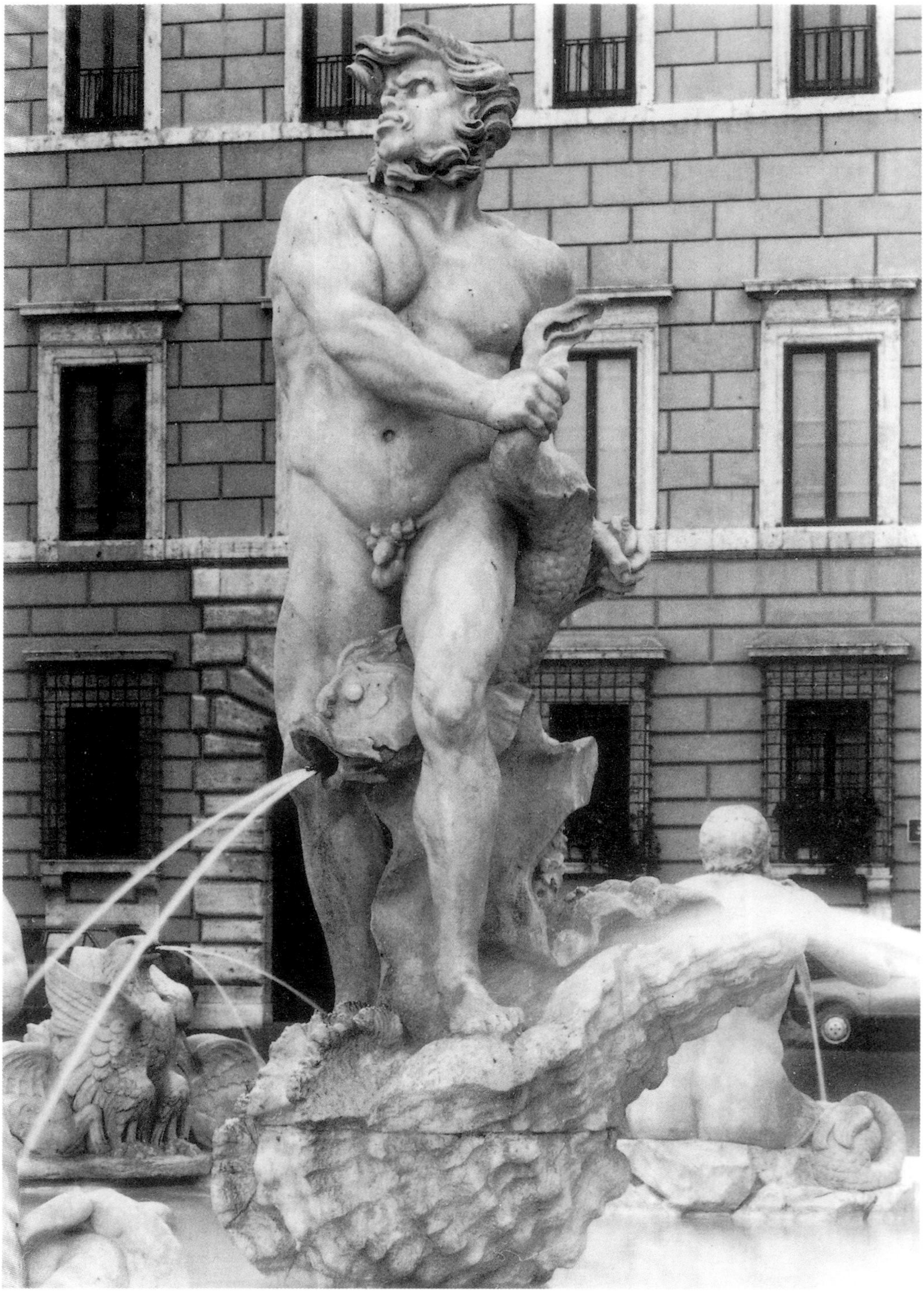

Fontana del Moro, detail (1635-1655), marble. Rome, Piazza Navona

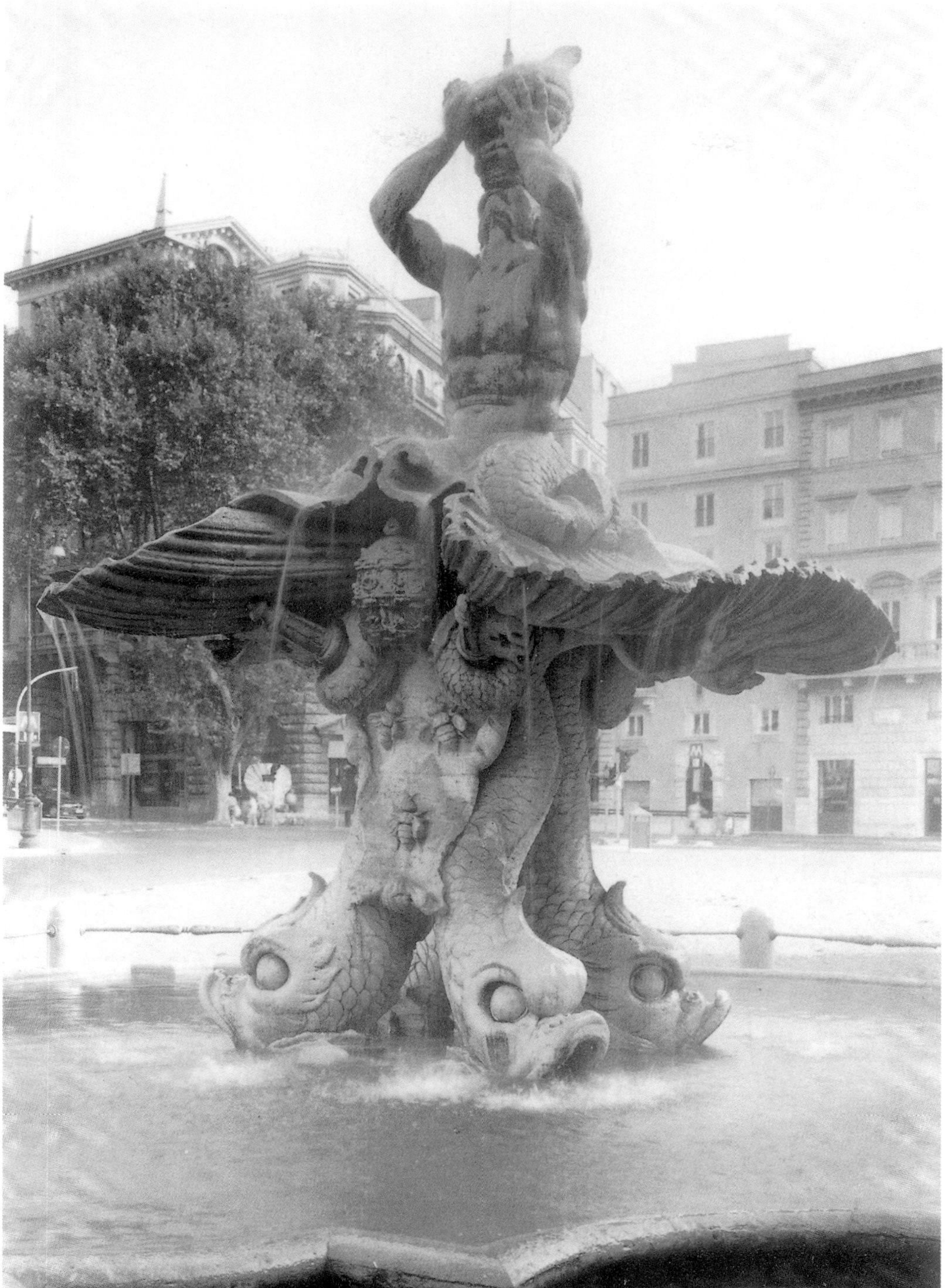

Triton Fountain (1637), travertine stone. Rome, Piazza Barberini

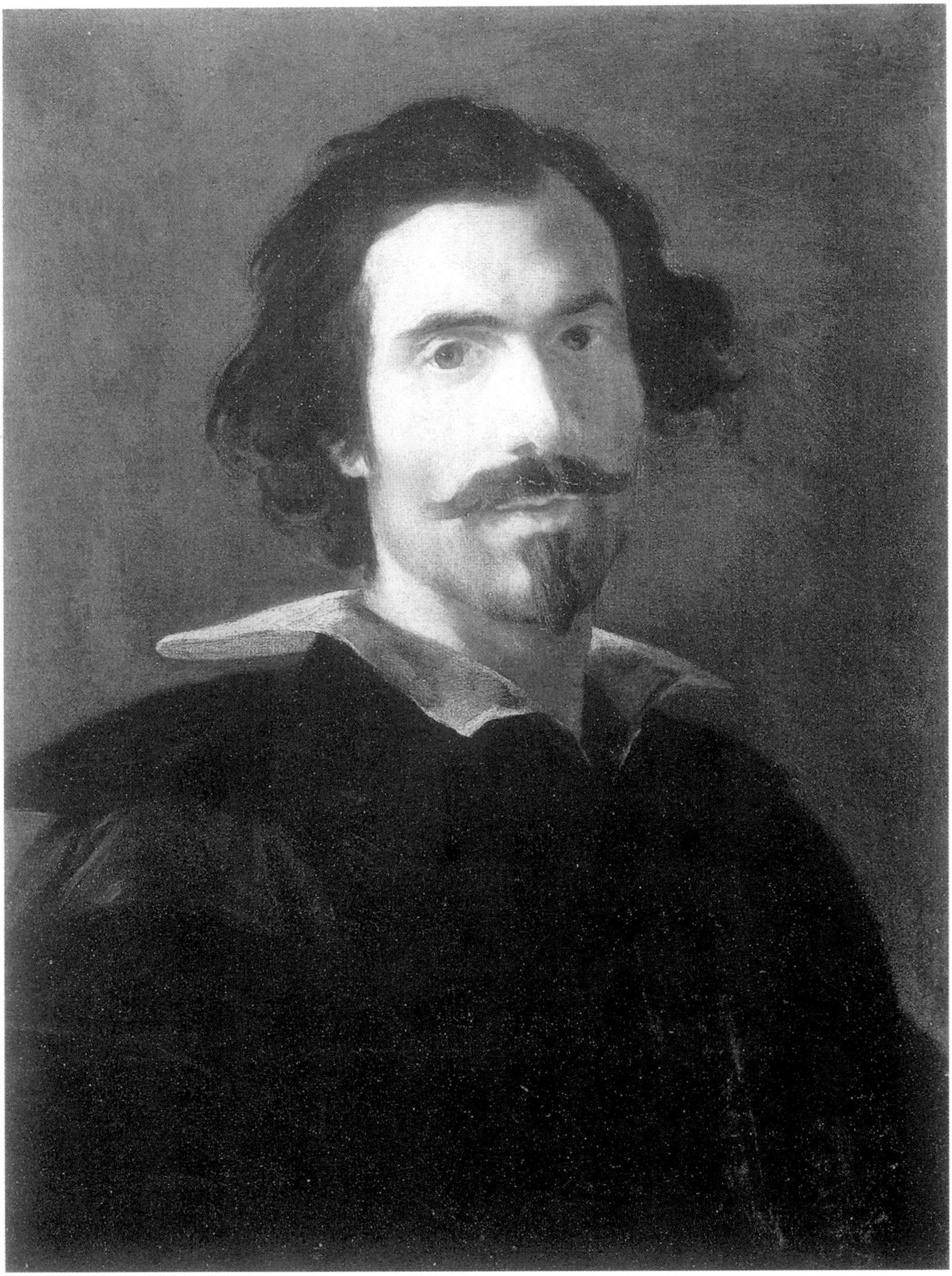

Self-portrait (1640 ca.), oil on canvas. Florence, Uffizi

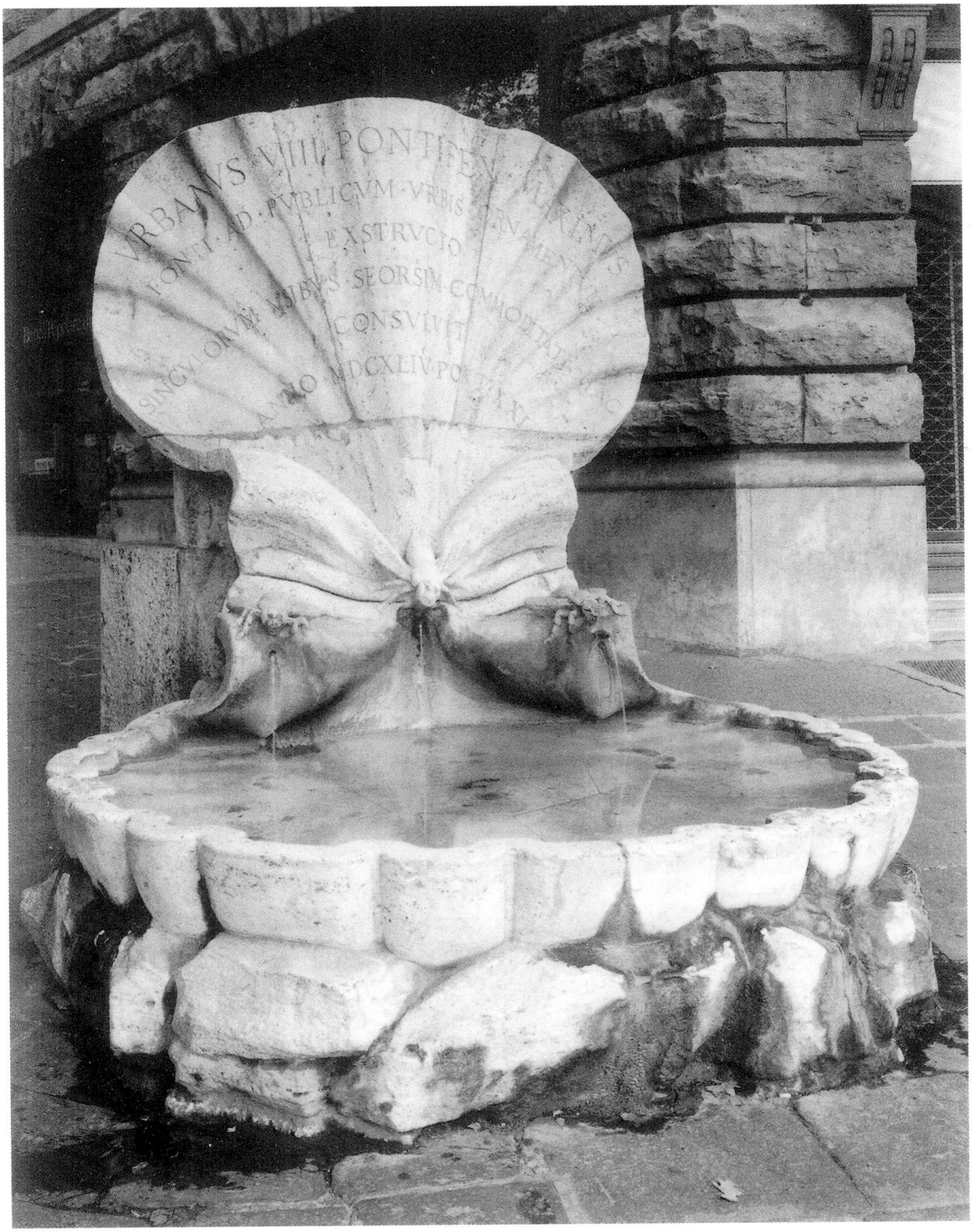

Fontana delle Api (1644), travertine stone. Rome, Piazza Barberini

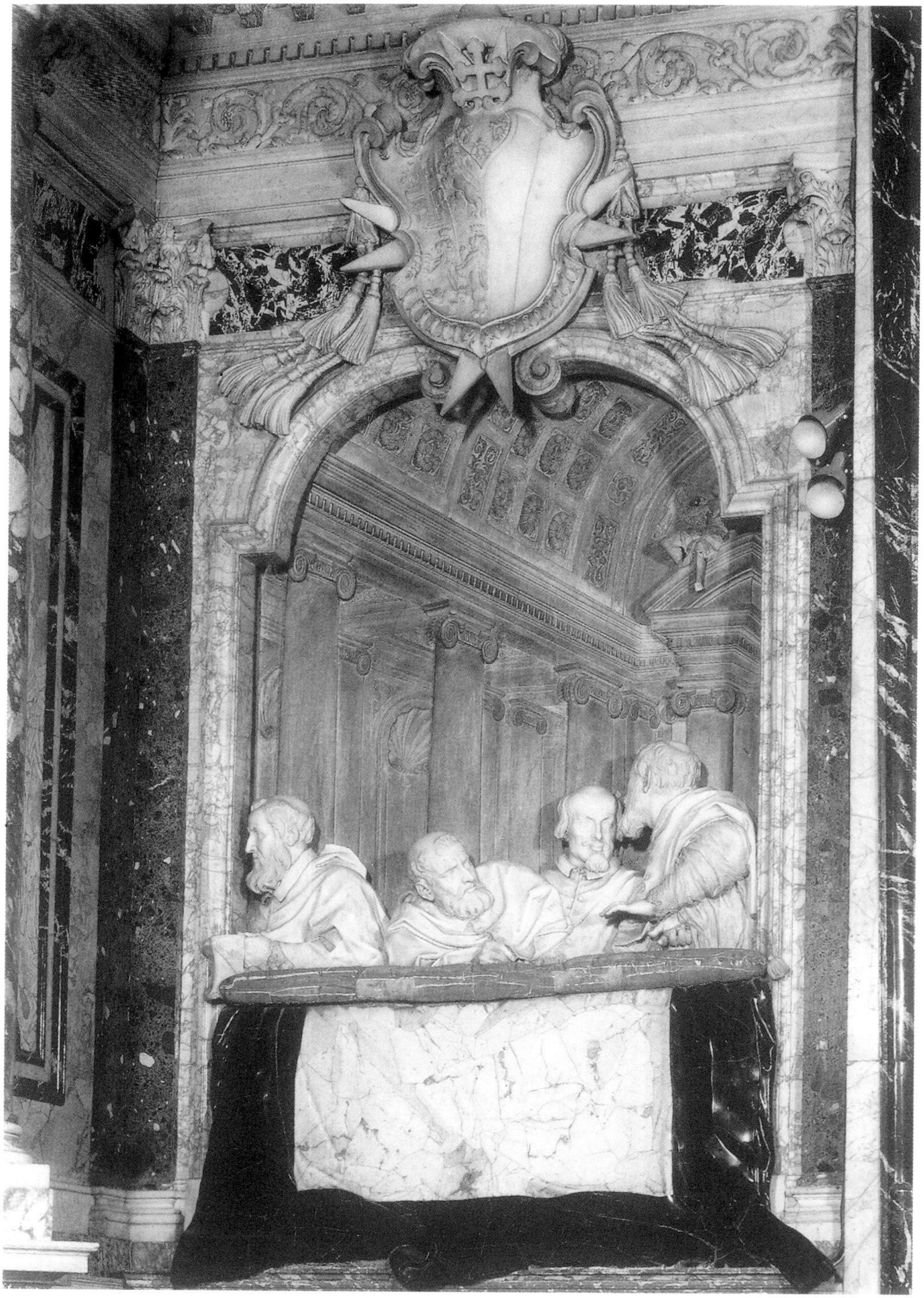

The Cornaro Family, detail (1645-1652), marble. Rome, Church of Santa Maria della Vittoria

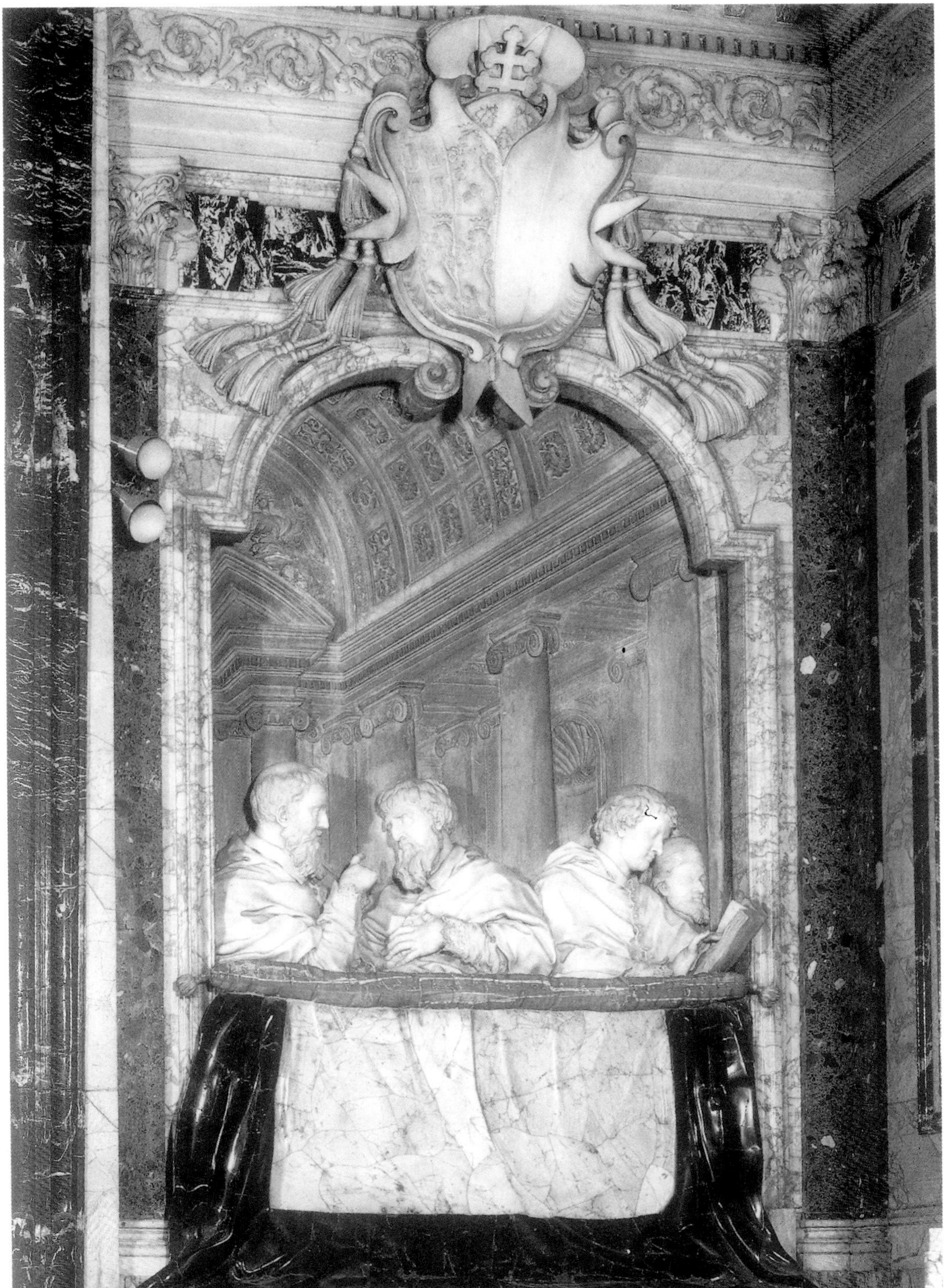

The Cornaro Family, detail (1645-1652), marble. Rome, Church of Santa Maria della Vittoria

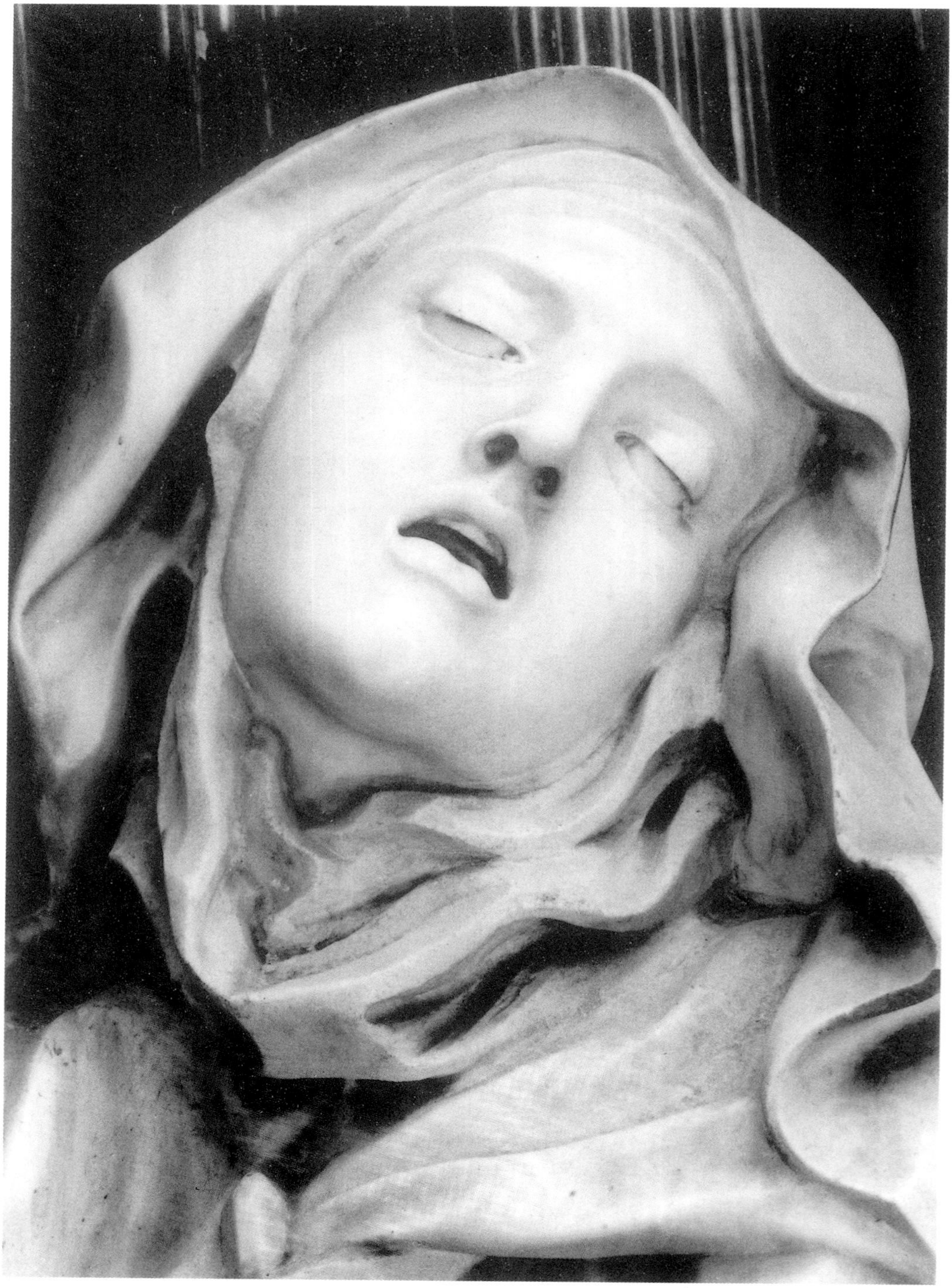

Ecstasy of St. Teresa, detail (1645-1652), marble group.
Rome, Church of Santa Maria della Vittoria

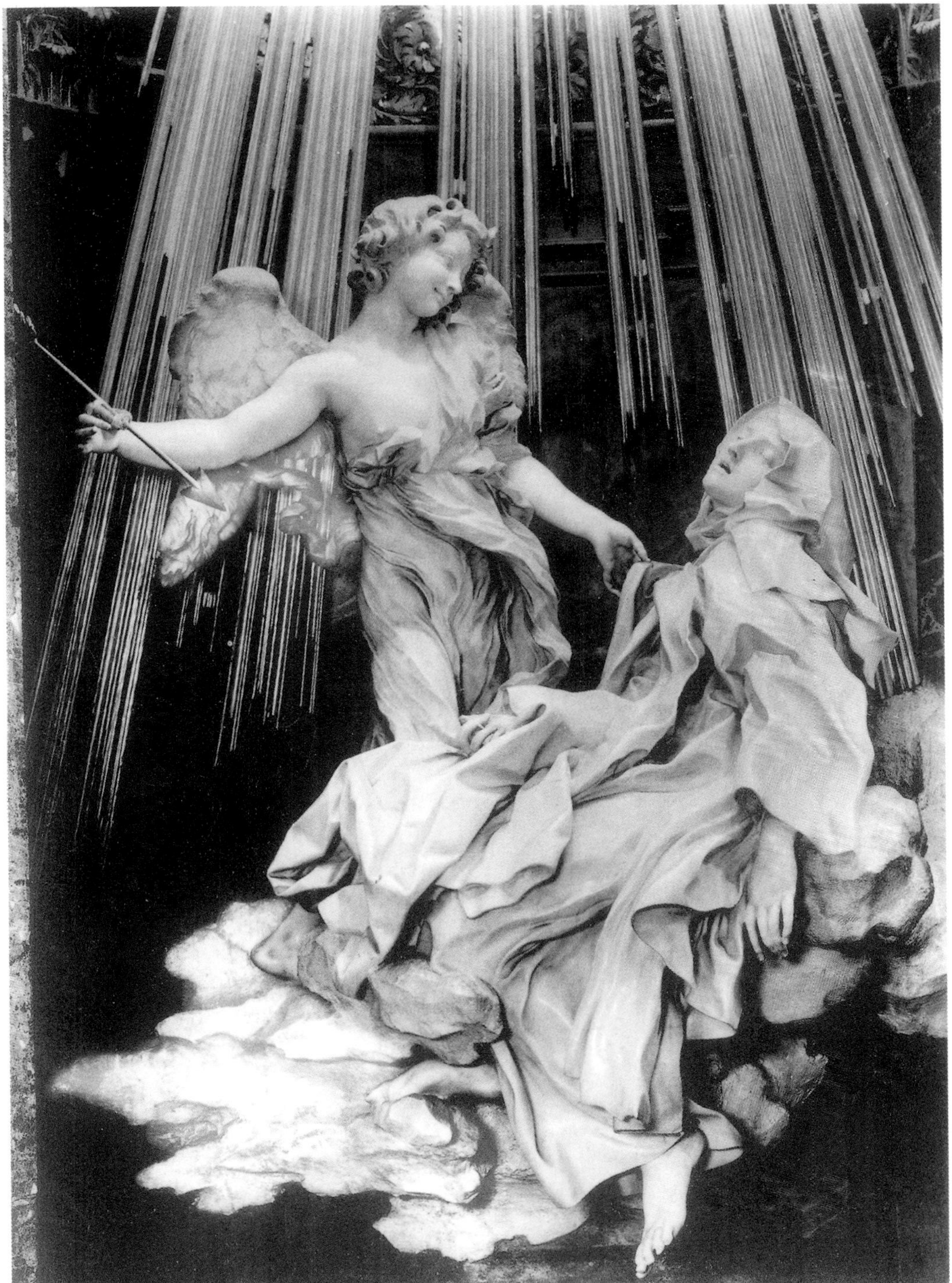

Ecstasy of St. Teresa, (1645-1652), marble group.
Rome, Church of Santa Maria della Vittoria

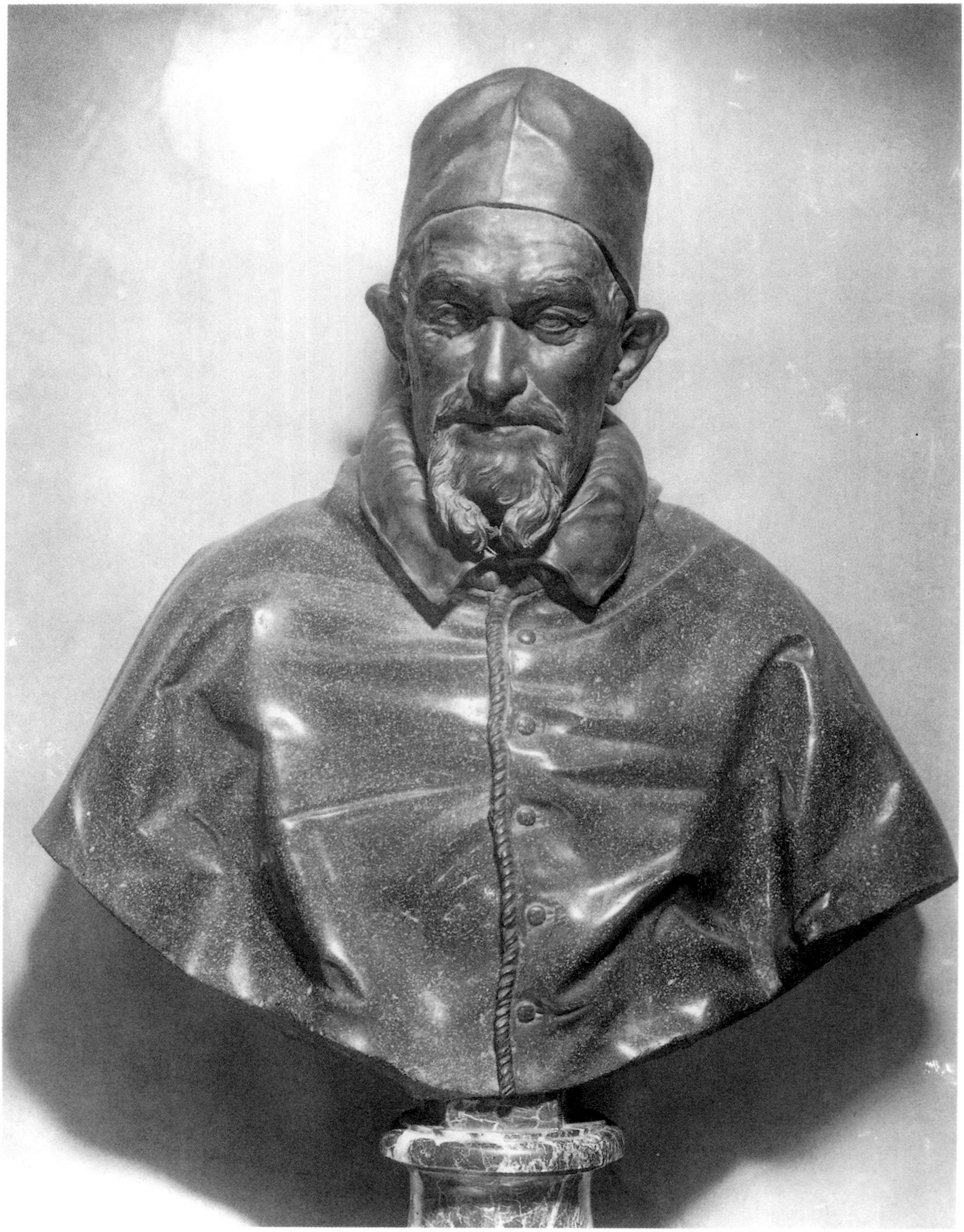

Innocent X (1647 ca.), porphyry. Rome, Galleria Doria Pamphili

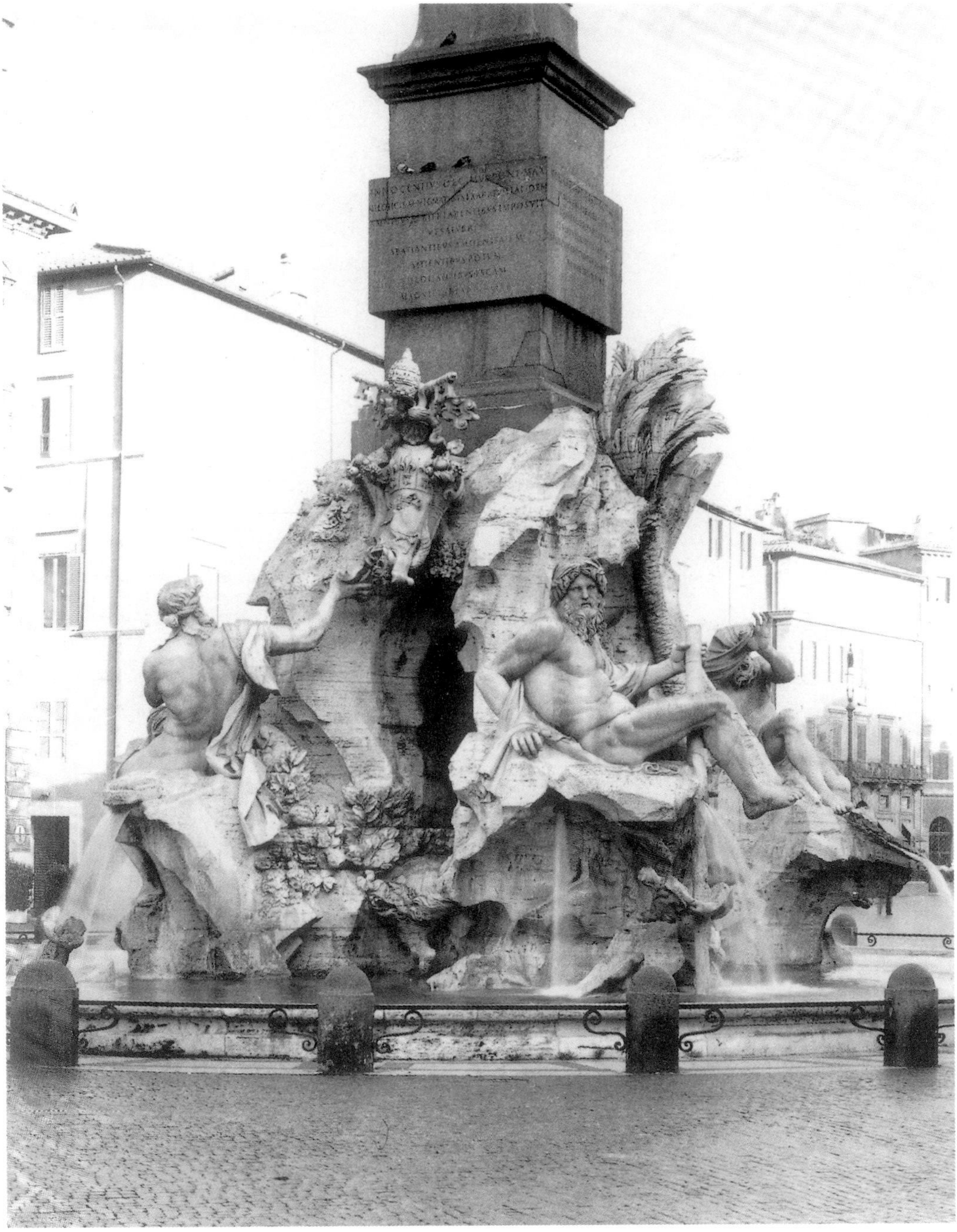

Four Rivers Fountain (1648-1651), travertine and marble. Rome, Piazza Navona

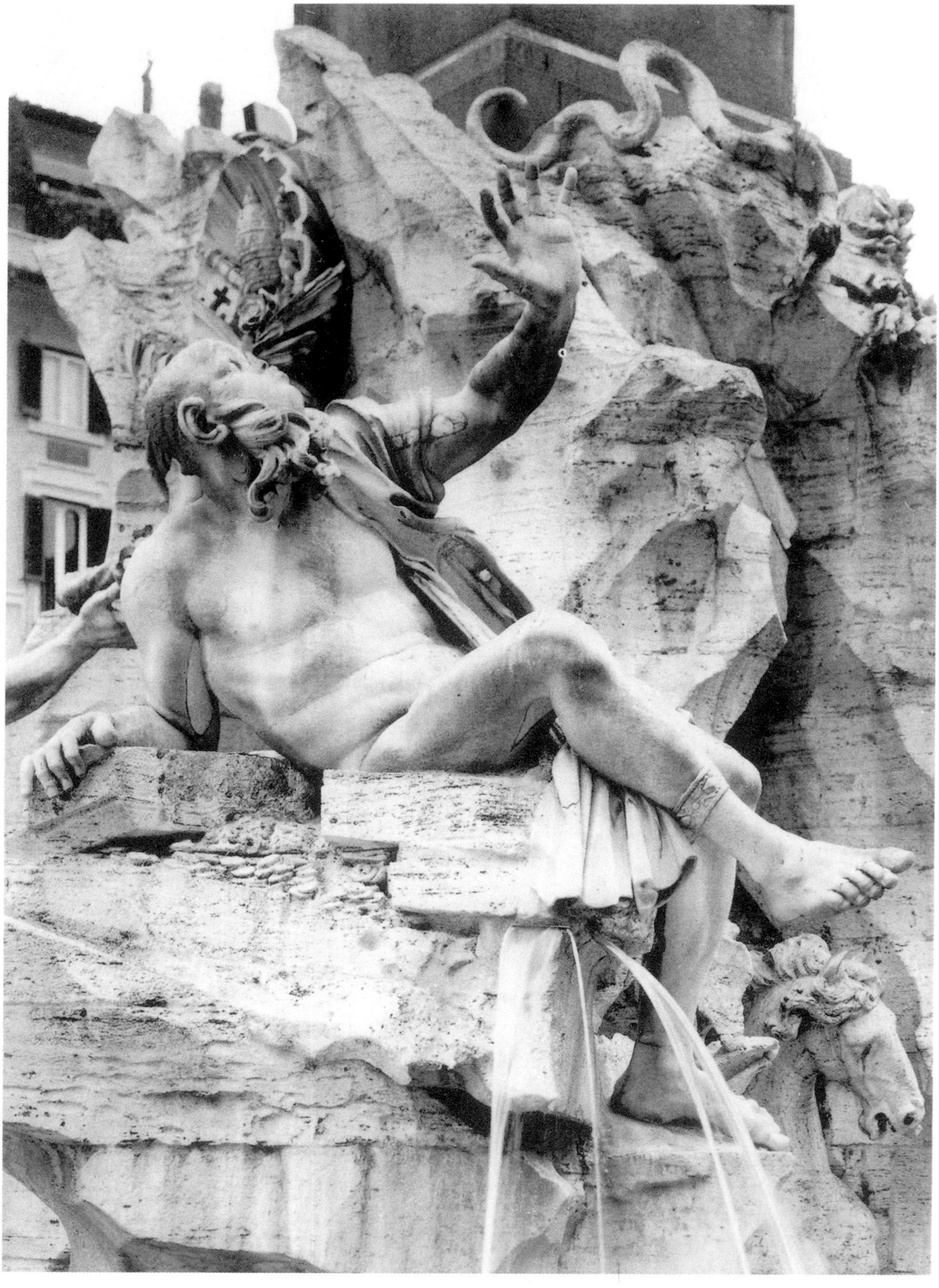

Four Rivers Fountain: the Rio de la Plata (1648-1651), travertine and marble. Rome, Piazza Navona

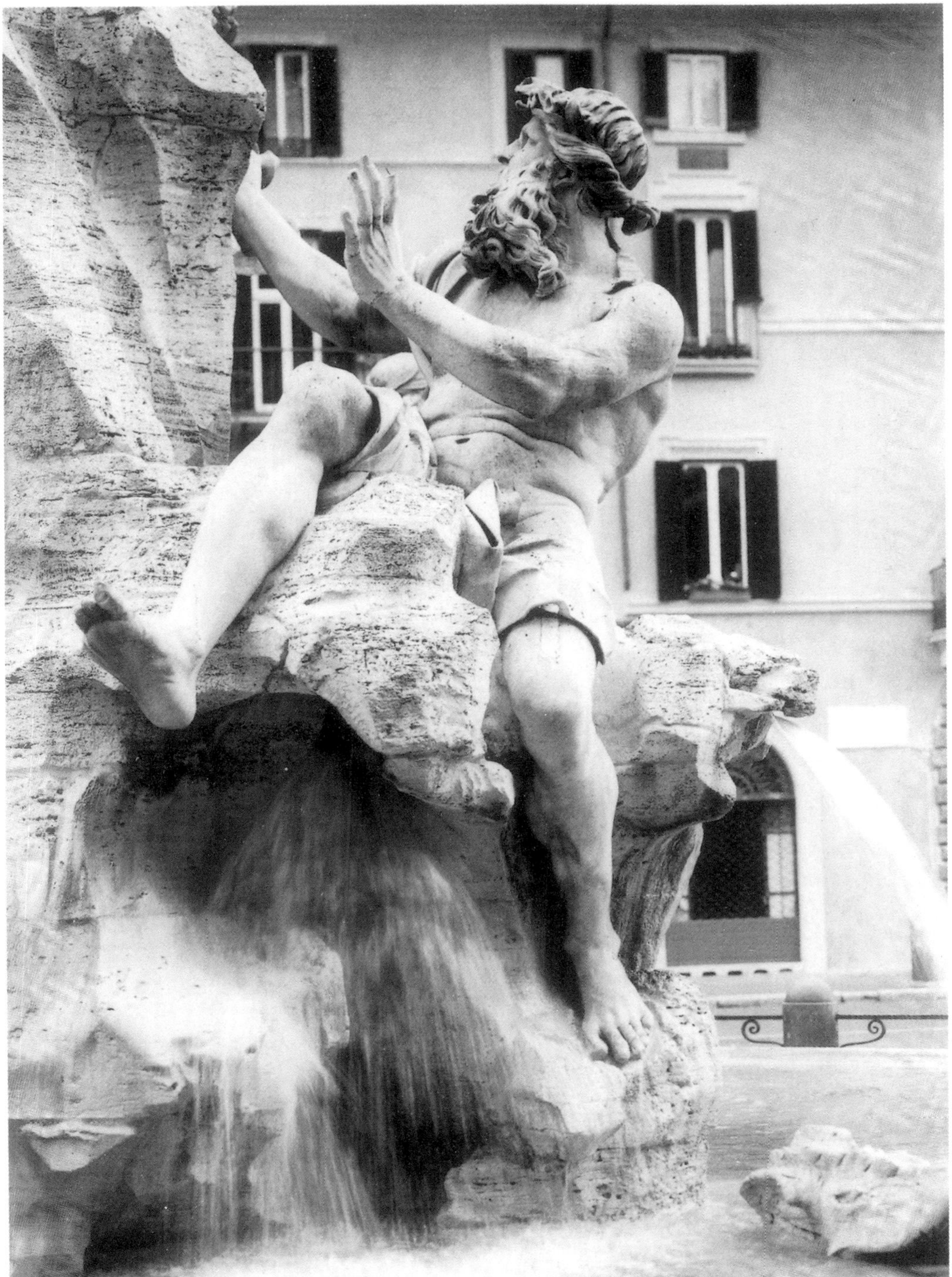

Four Rivers Fountain: the Danube River (1648-1651), travertine and marble.
Rome, Piazza Navona

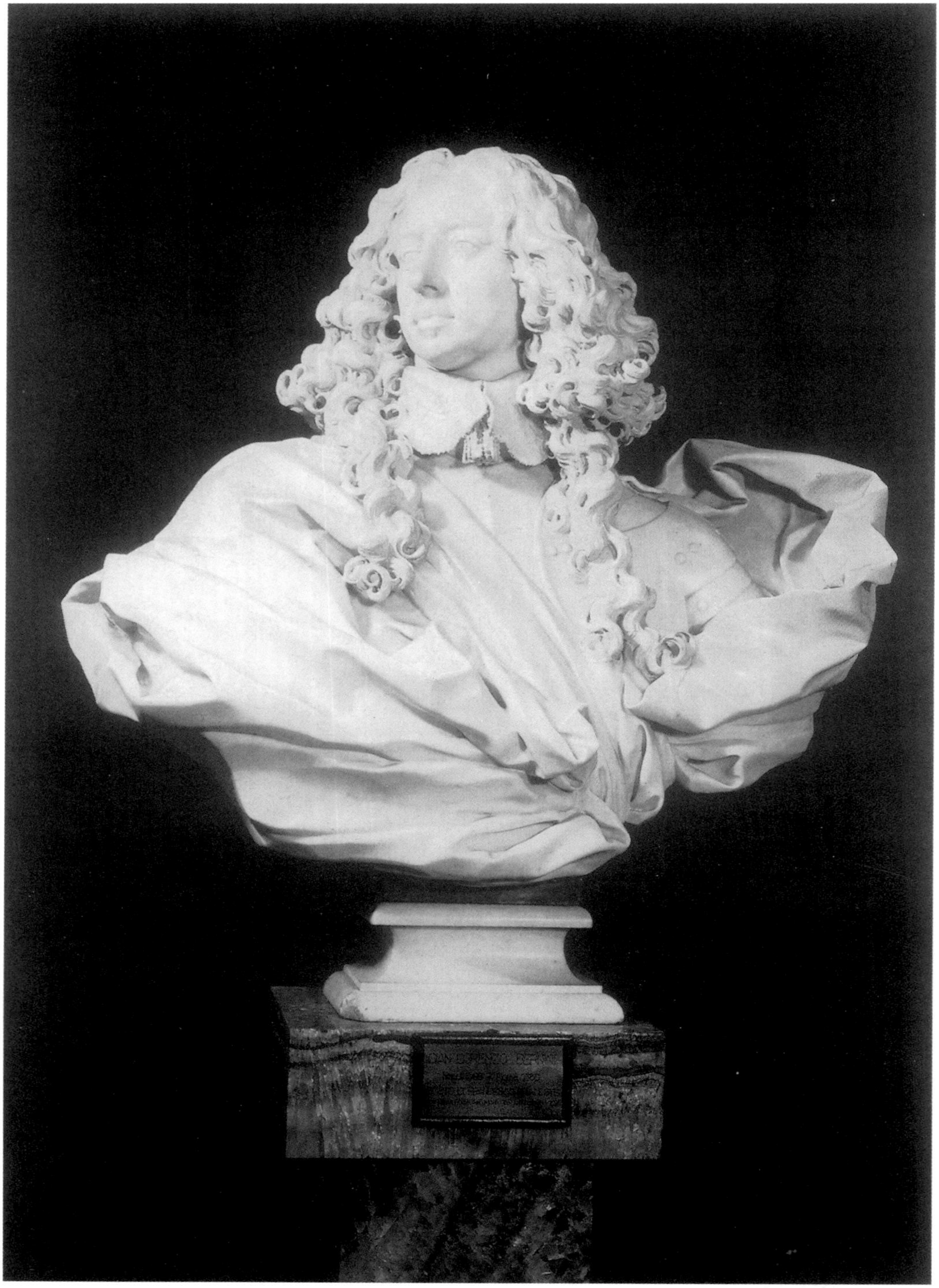

Francesco I d'Este (1650-1651), marble. Modena, Museo Estense

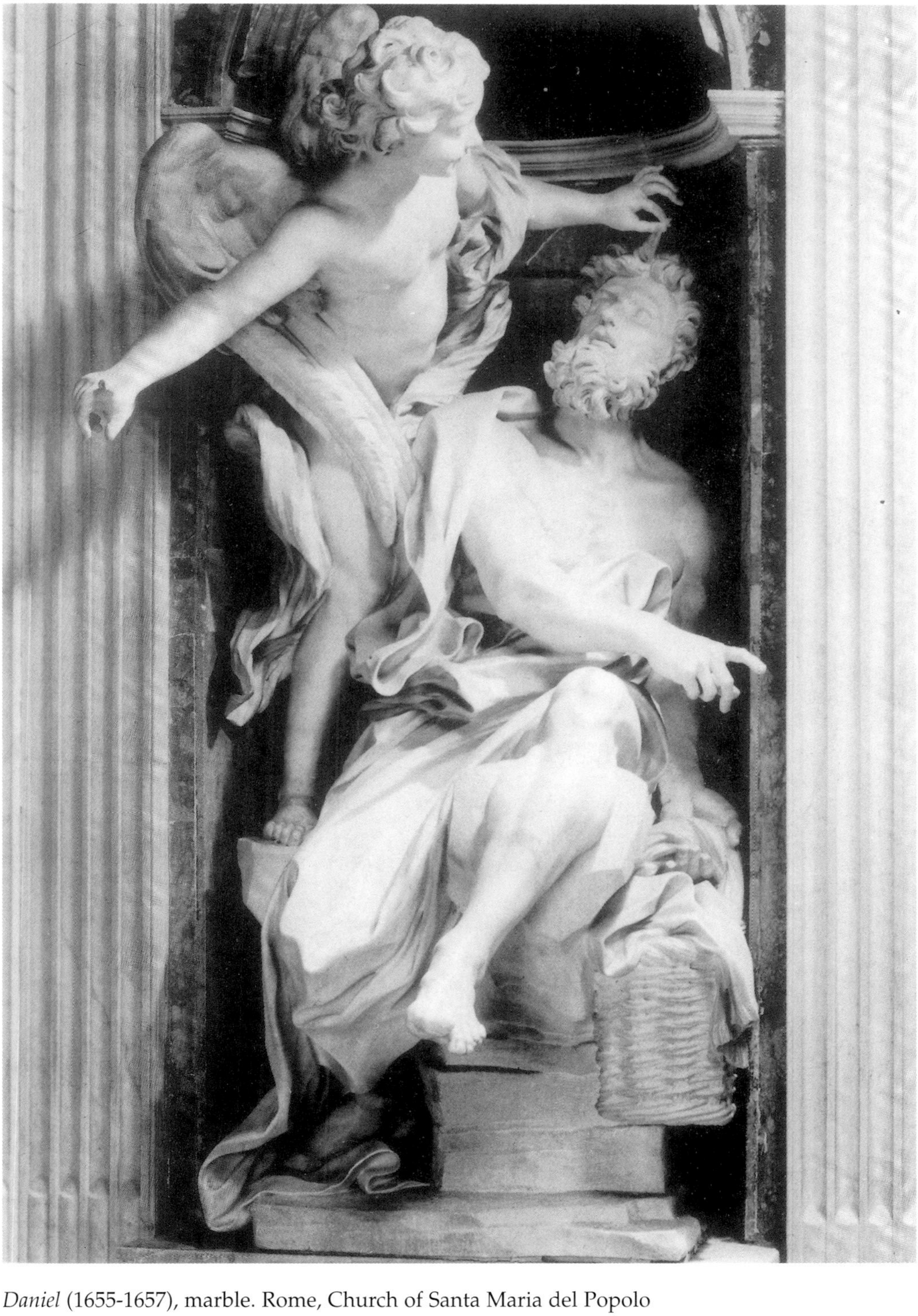

Daniel (1655-1657), marble. Rome, Church of Santa Maria del Popolo

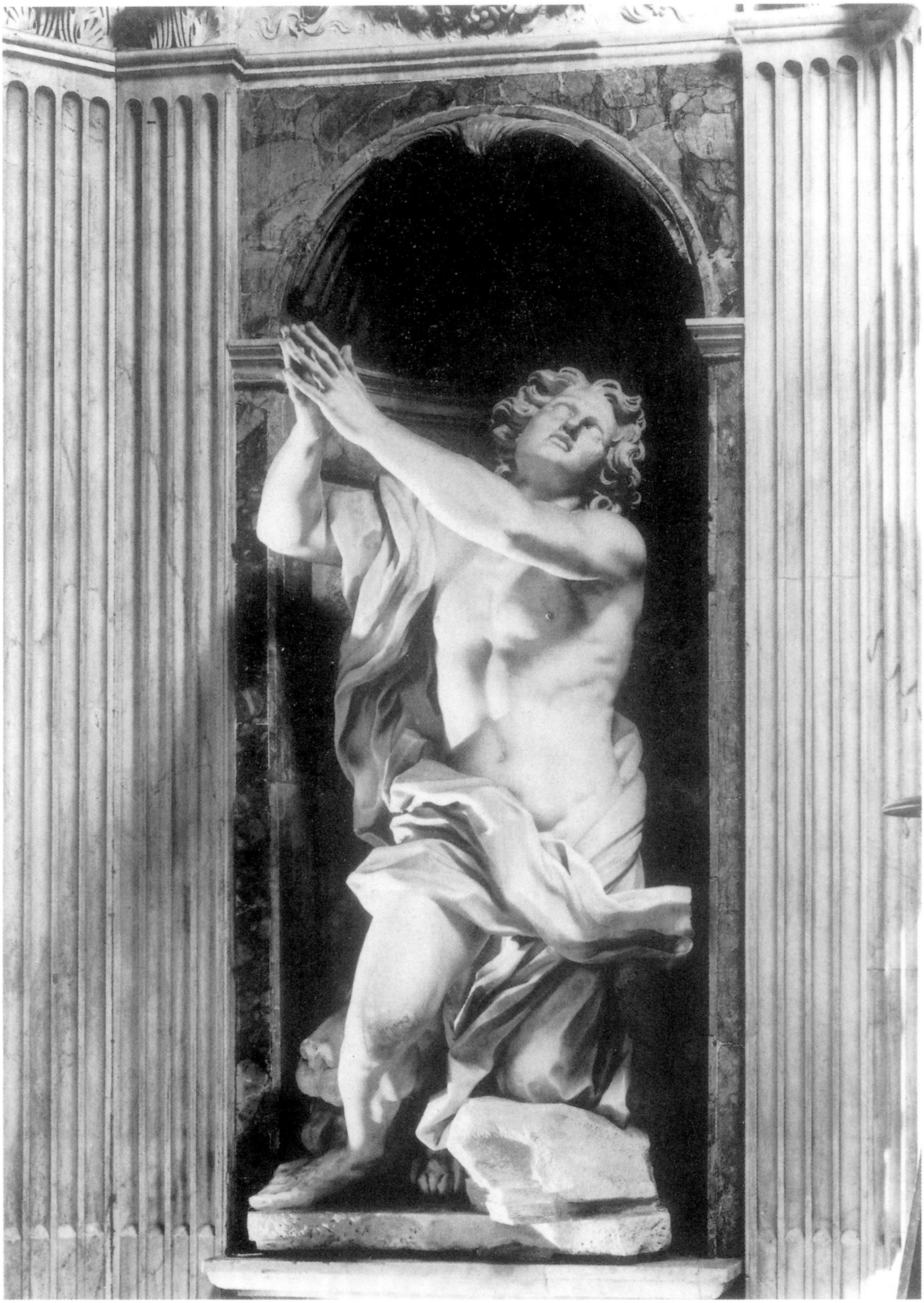

Habakkuk (1655-1657), marble. Rome, Church of Santa Maria del Popolo

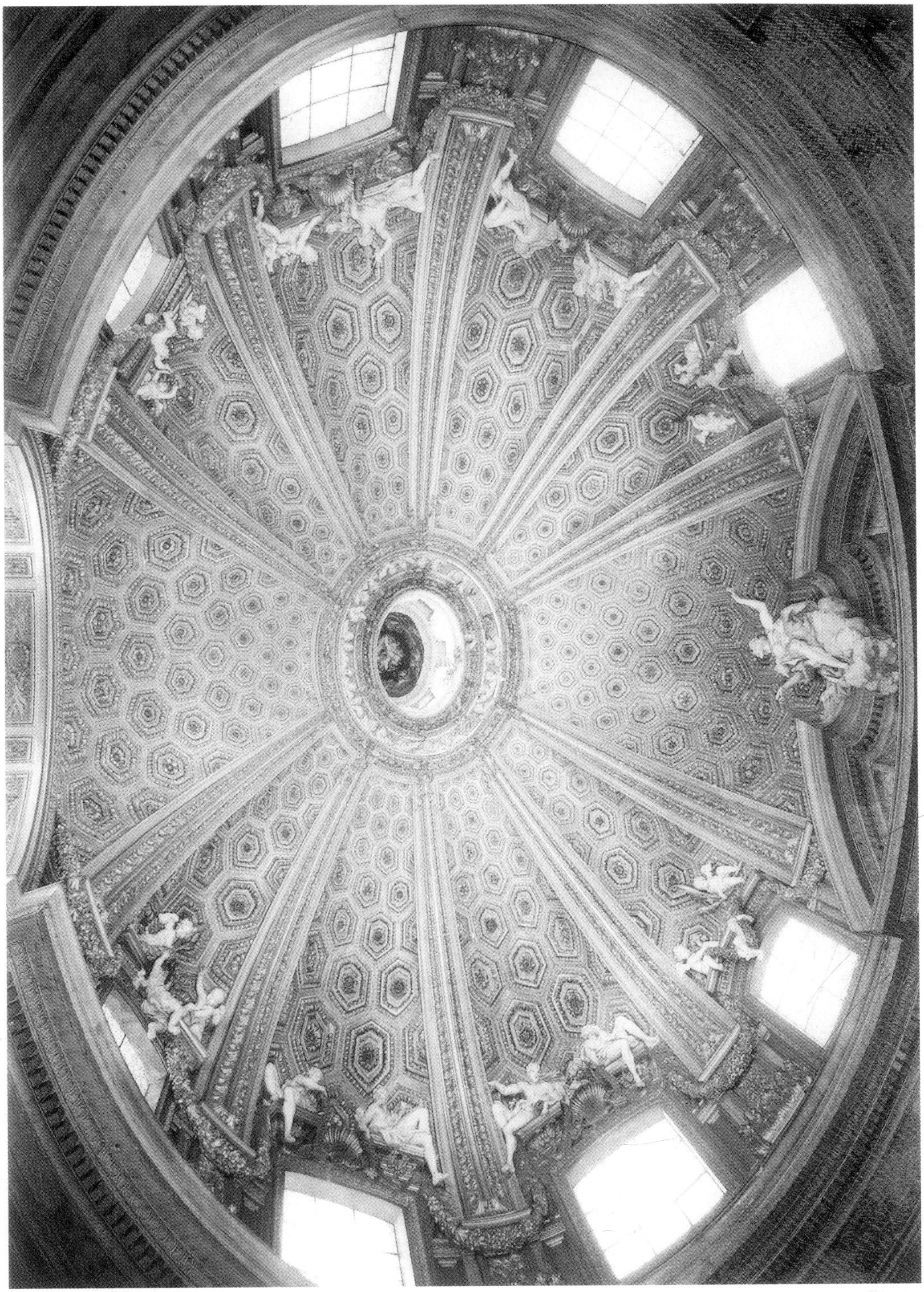

Dome (1658-1665). Rome, Church of Sant'Andrea al Quirinale

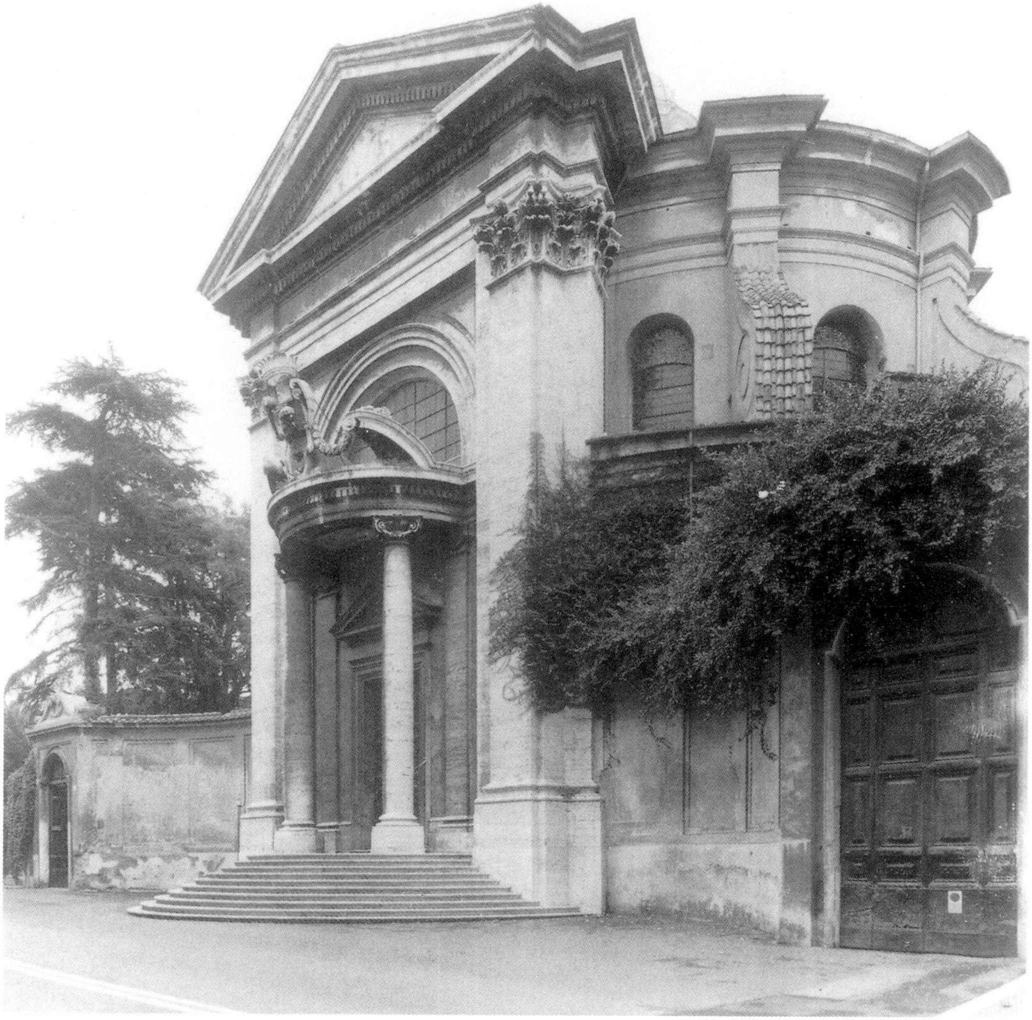

Facade (1658-1665). Rome, Church of Sant'Andrea al Quirinale

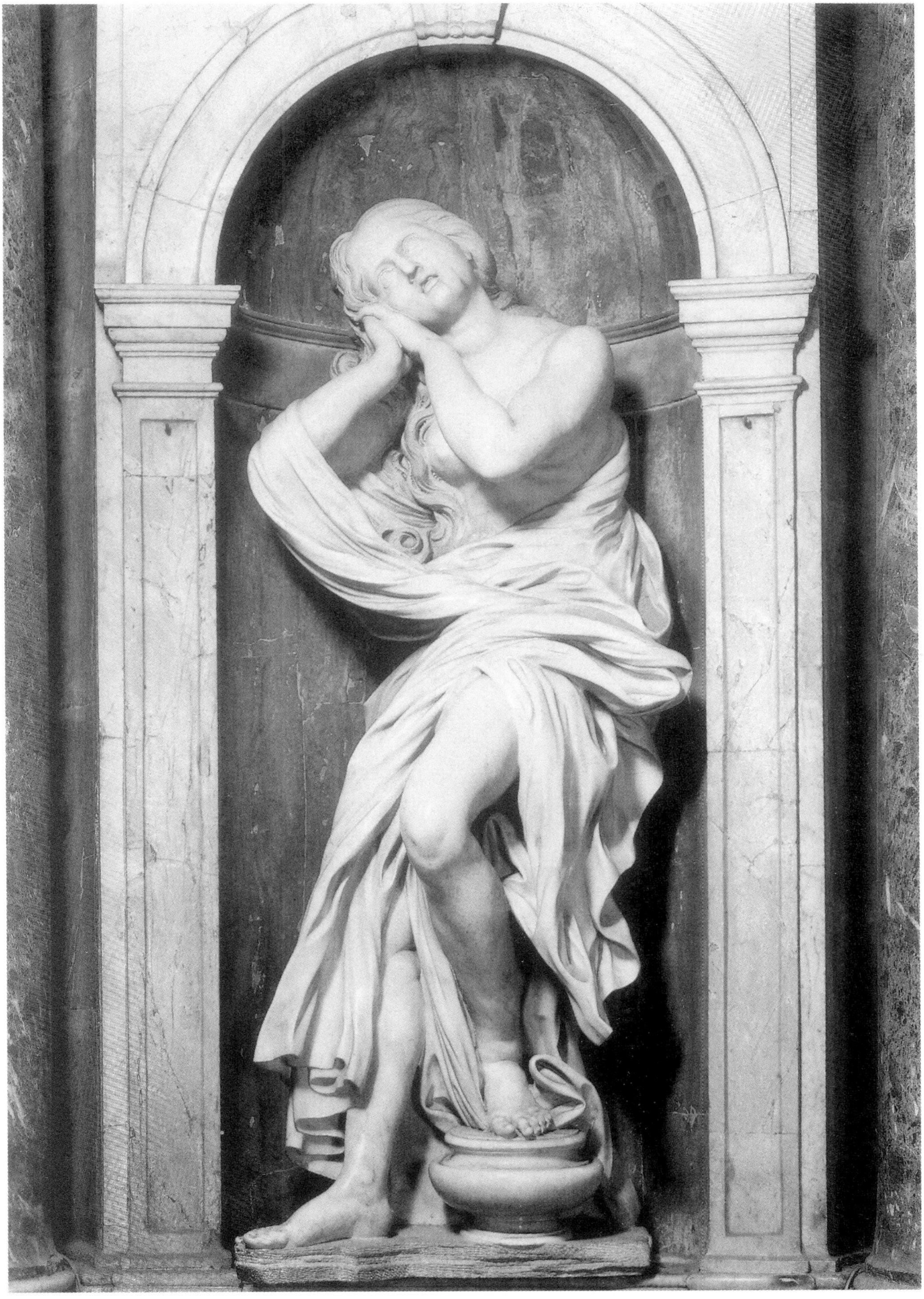

Mary Magdalen (1661), marble. Siena, Cathedral

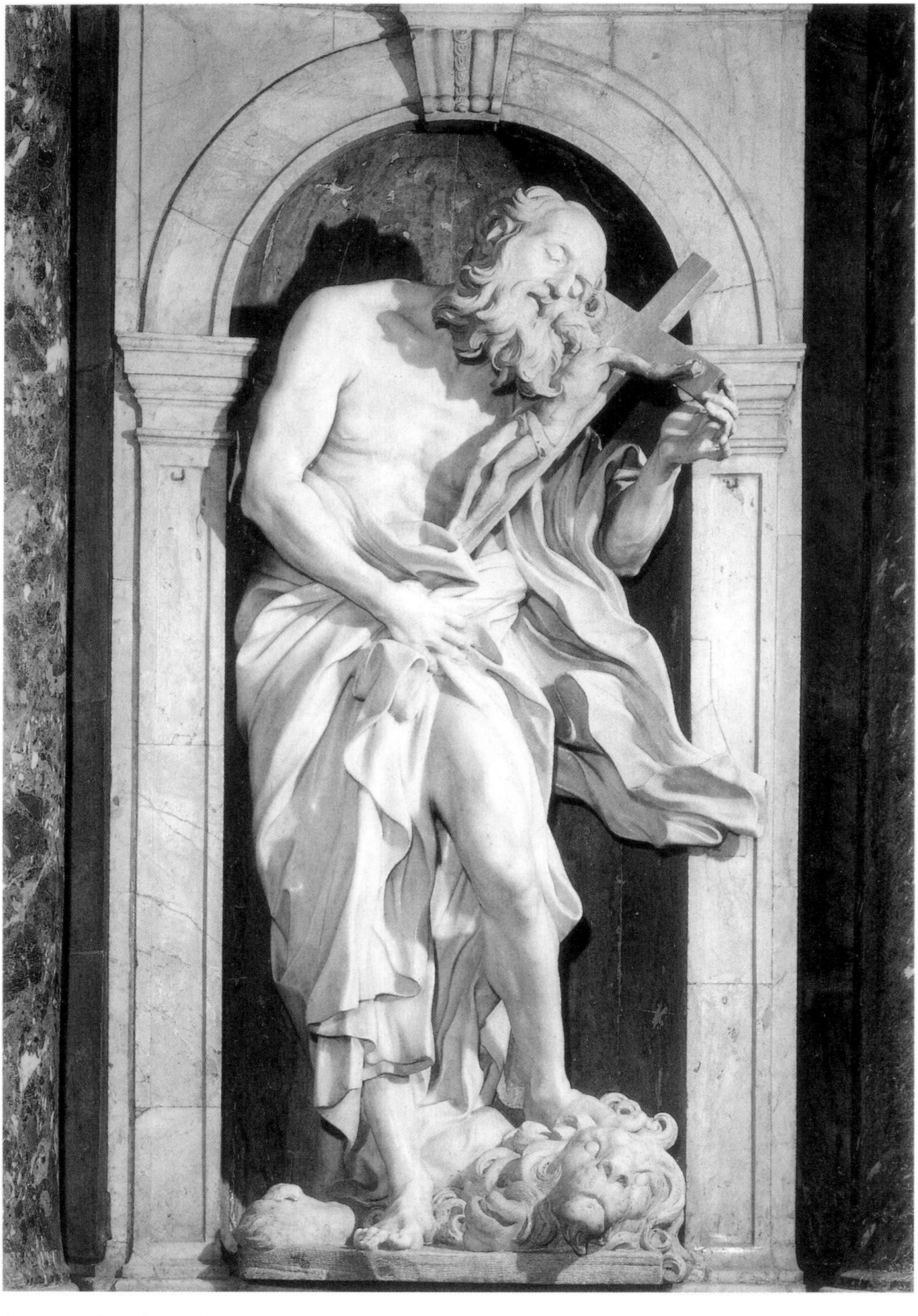

St. Jerome (1663) marble. Siena, Cathedral

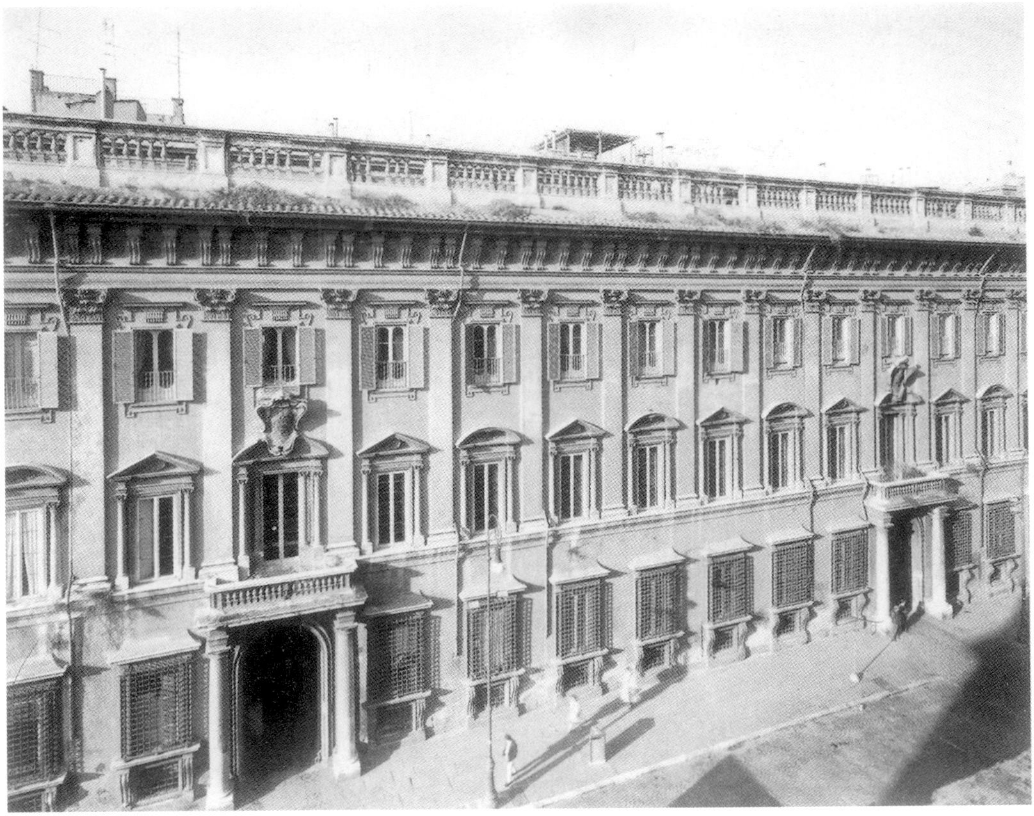

Facade (1665). Rome, Palazzo Chigi (now Odescalchi)

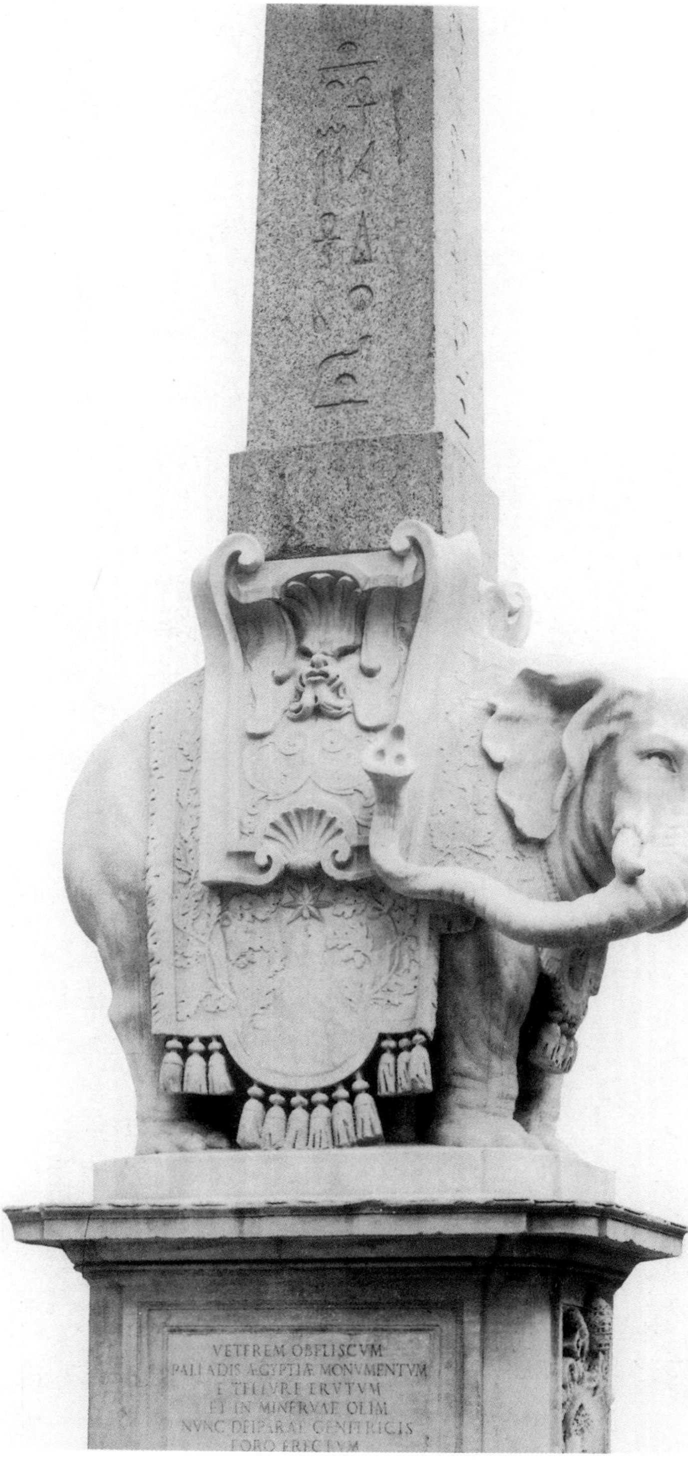

Elephant (1666-1667), marble. Rome, Piazza della Minerva

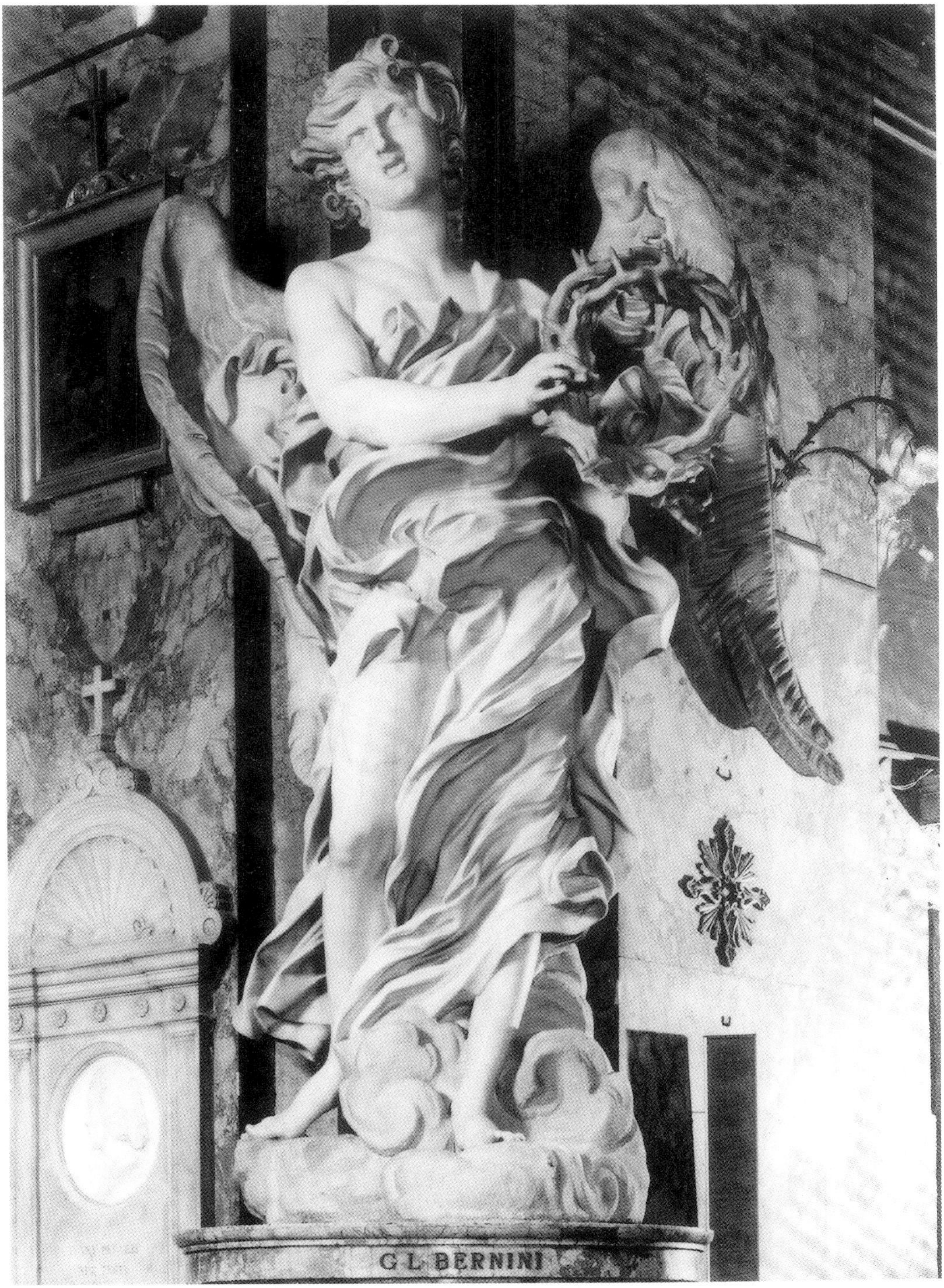

Angel with crown of thorns (1667-1669), marble. Rome, Church of Sant'Andrea delle Fratte

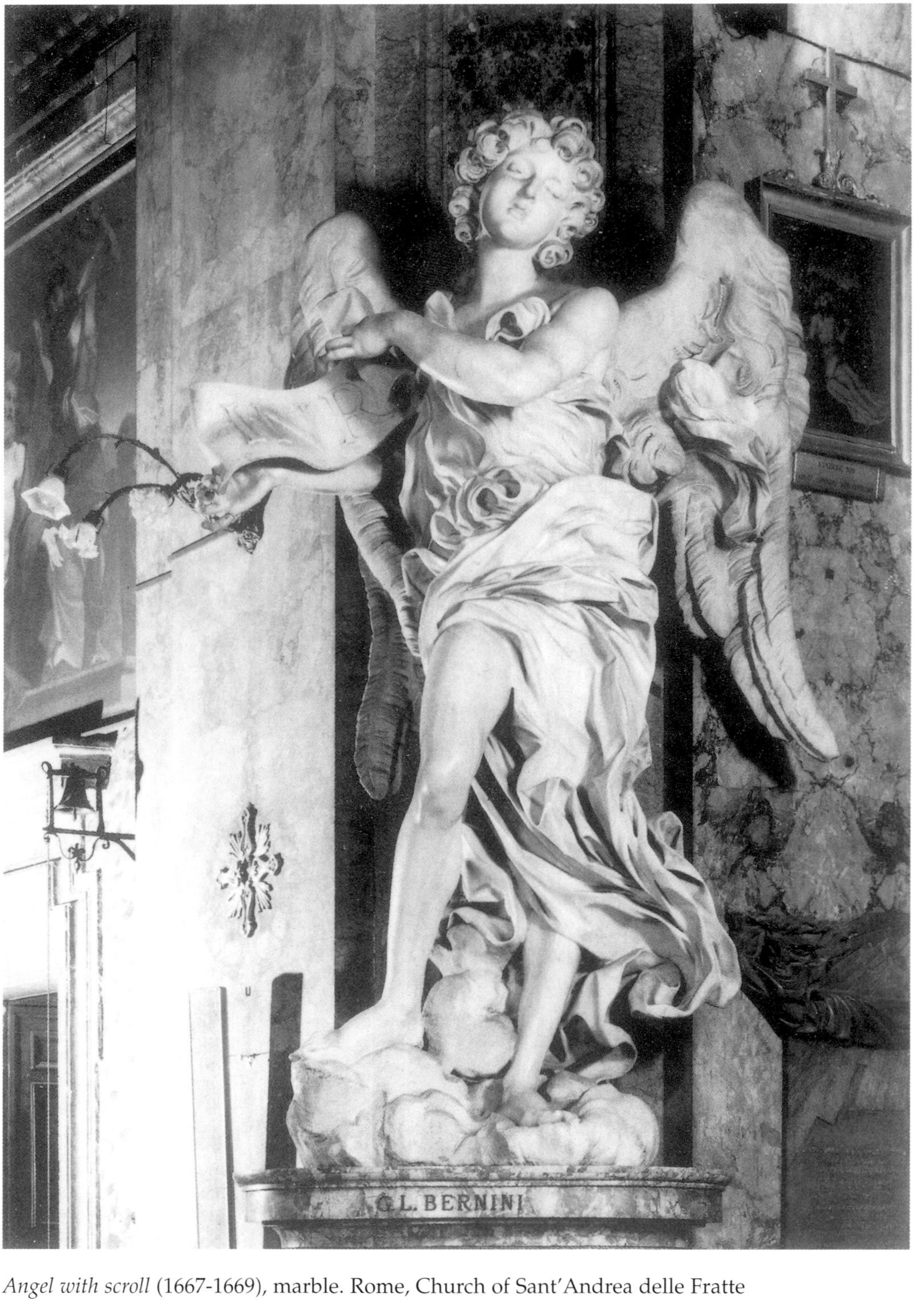

Angel with scroll (1667-1669), marble. Rome, Church of Sant'Andrea delle Fratte

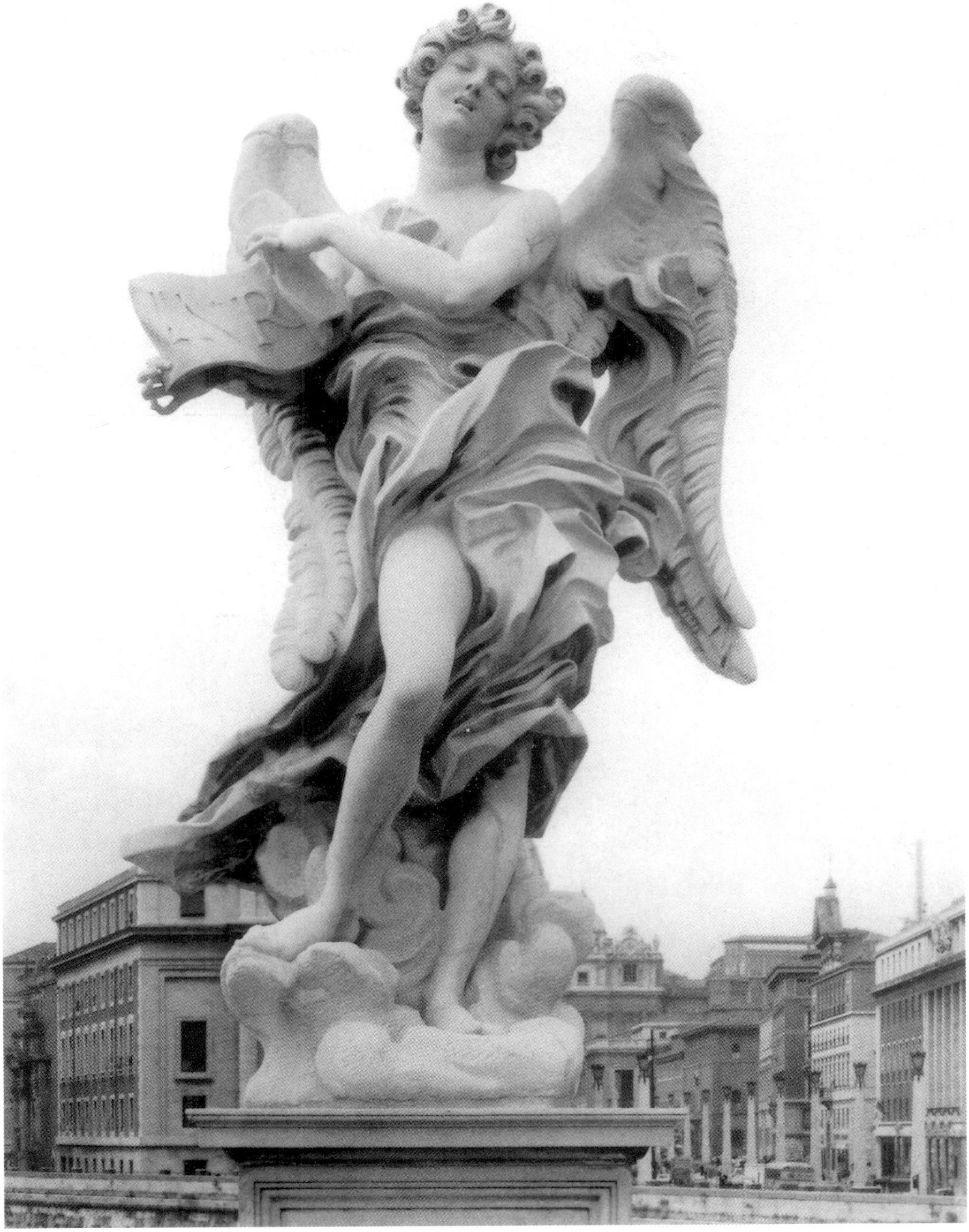

Angel with scroll, copy made by Cartari, marble. Rome, Ponte Sant'Angelo

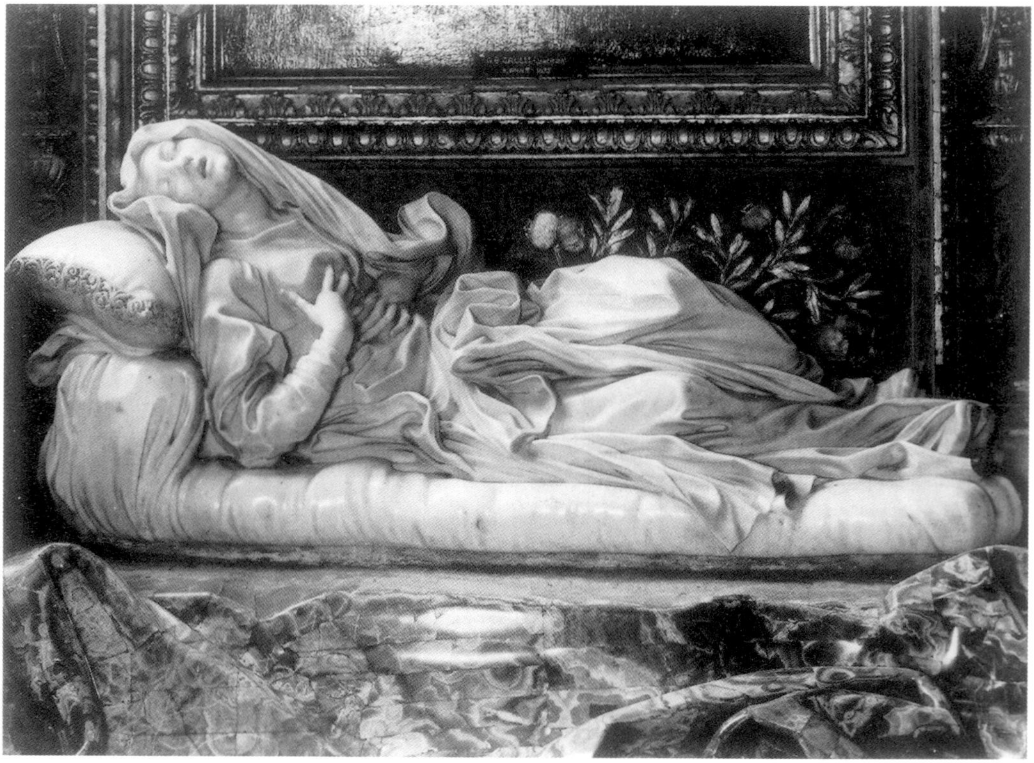

Blessed Ludovica Albertoni (1671-1674), marble and jasper.
Rome, Church of San Francesco a Ripa

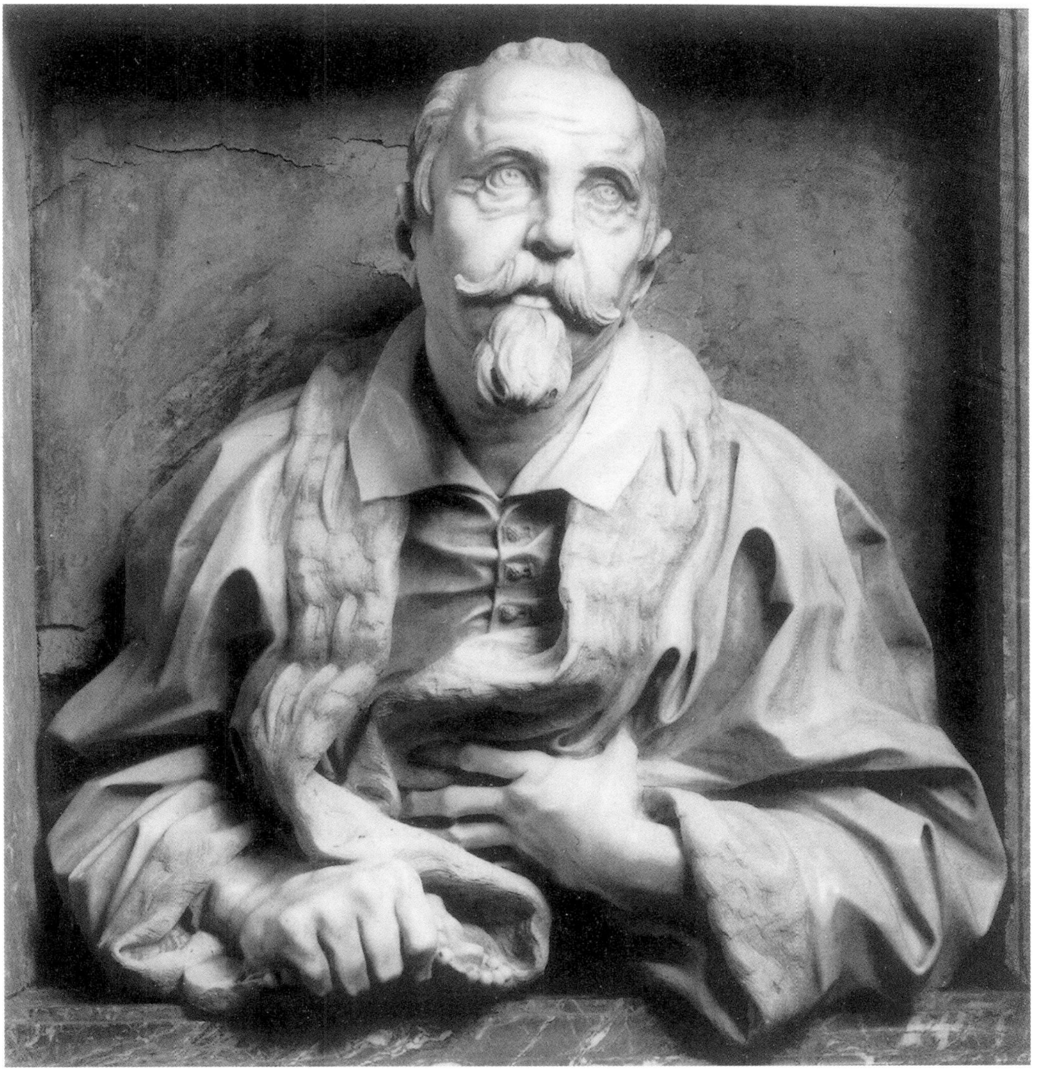

Gabriele Fonseca (1668-1675), marble. Rome, Church of San Lorenzo in Lucina

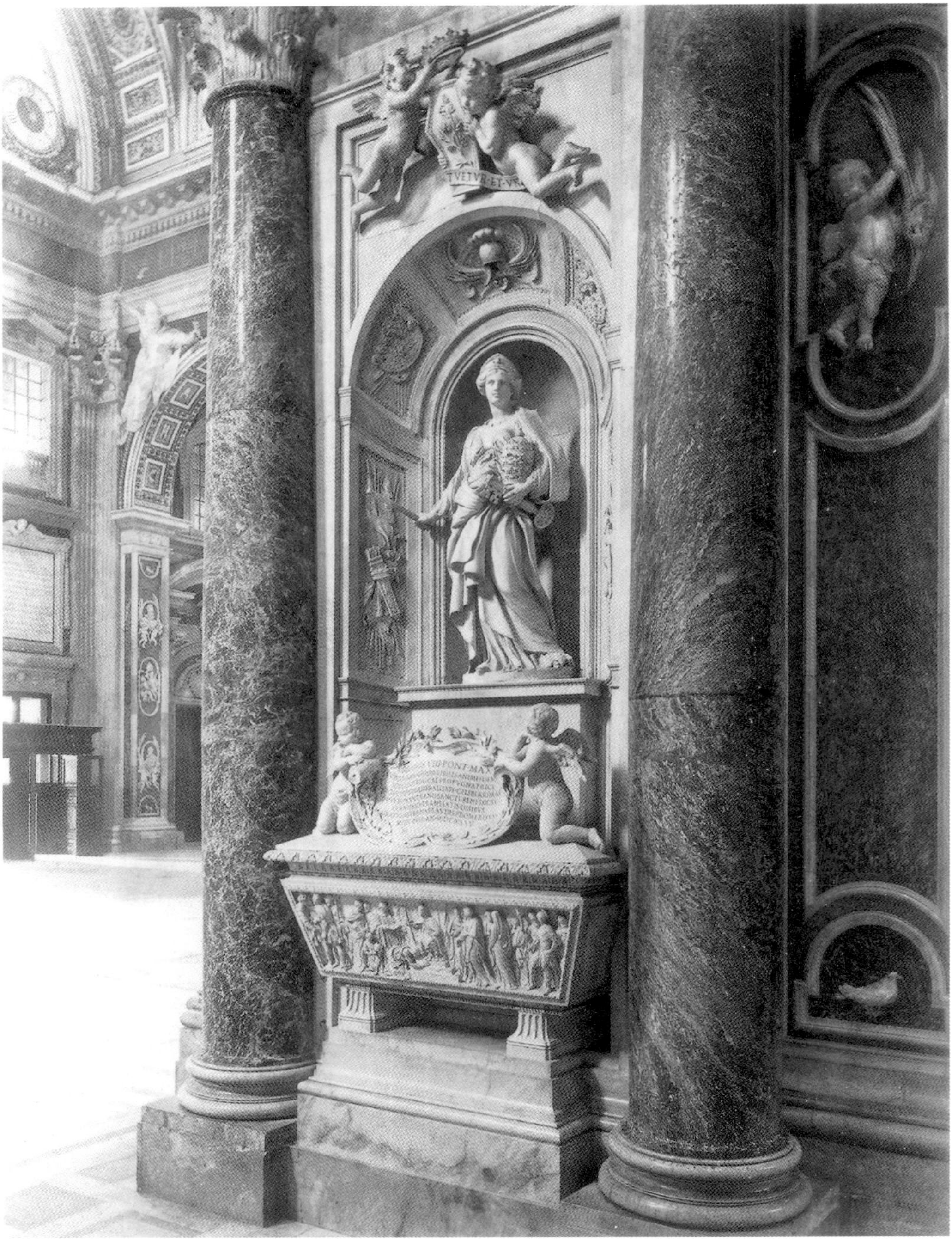

Tomb of Countess Matilde (1633-1637), marble. Vatican City, Basilica of St. Peter

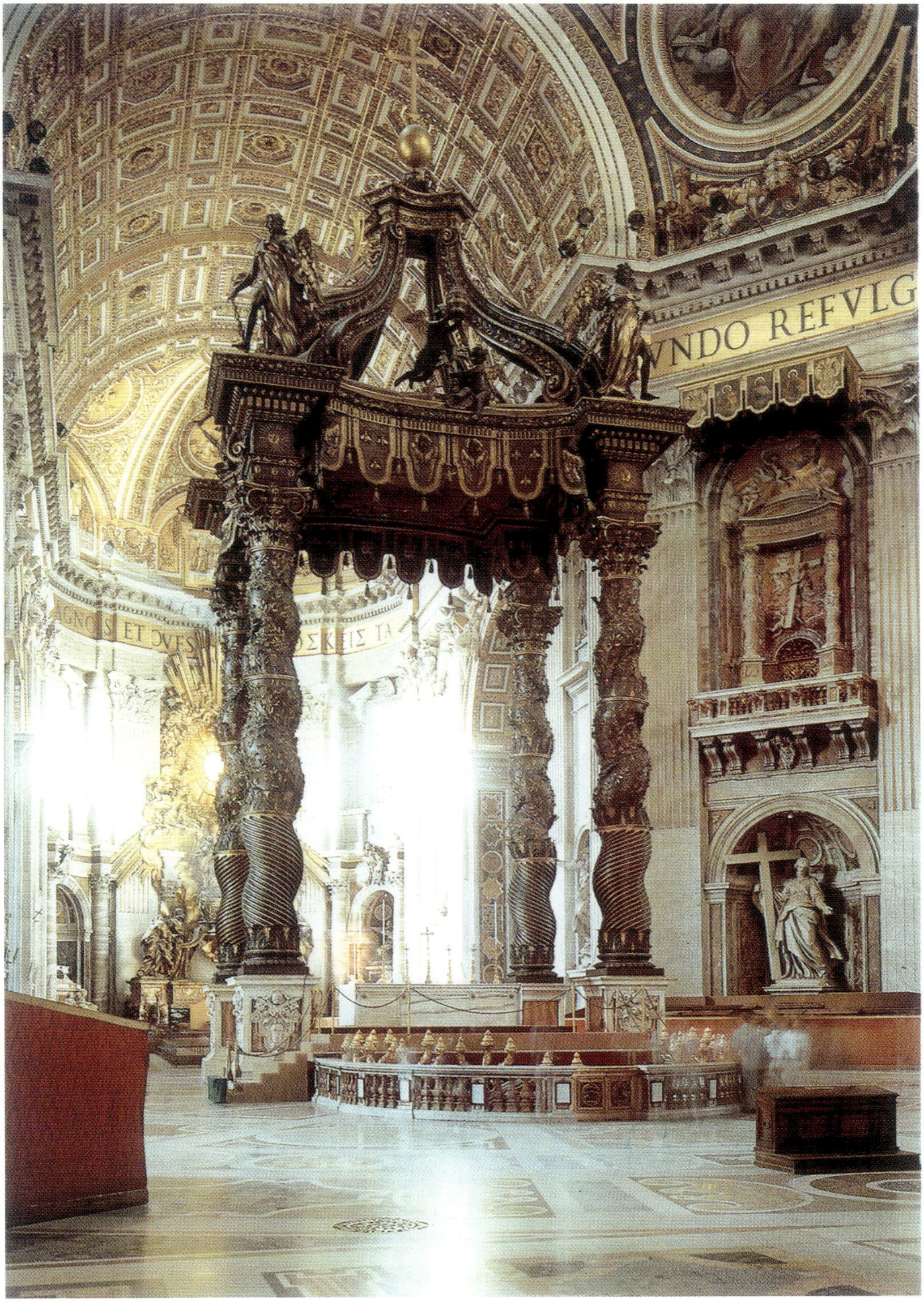

Baldachin (1624-1633), gilded bronze, wood and marble. Vatican City, Basilica of St. Peter

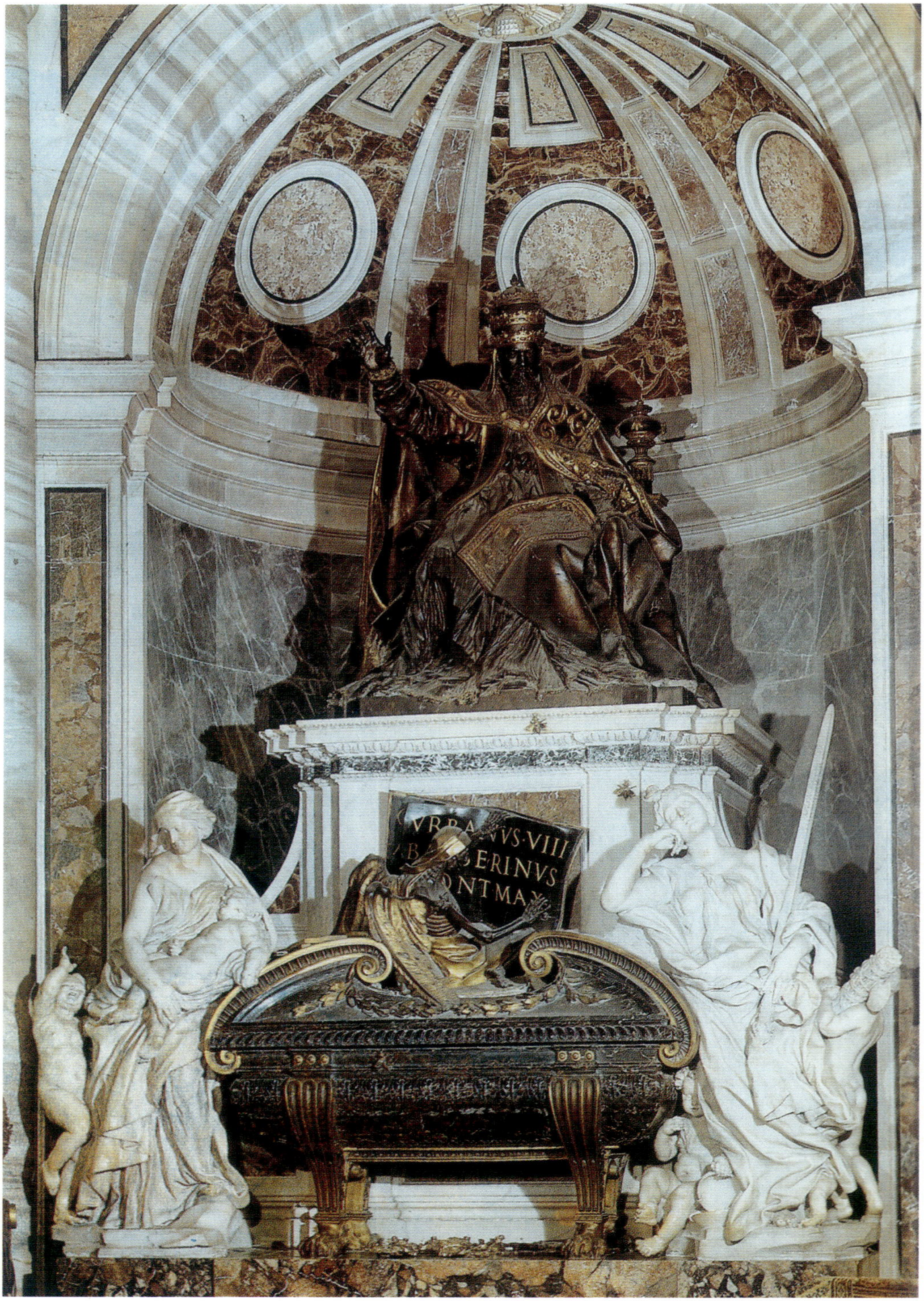

Tomb of Urban VIII (1628-1647), bronze and marble. Vatican City, Basilica of St. Peter

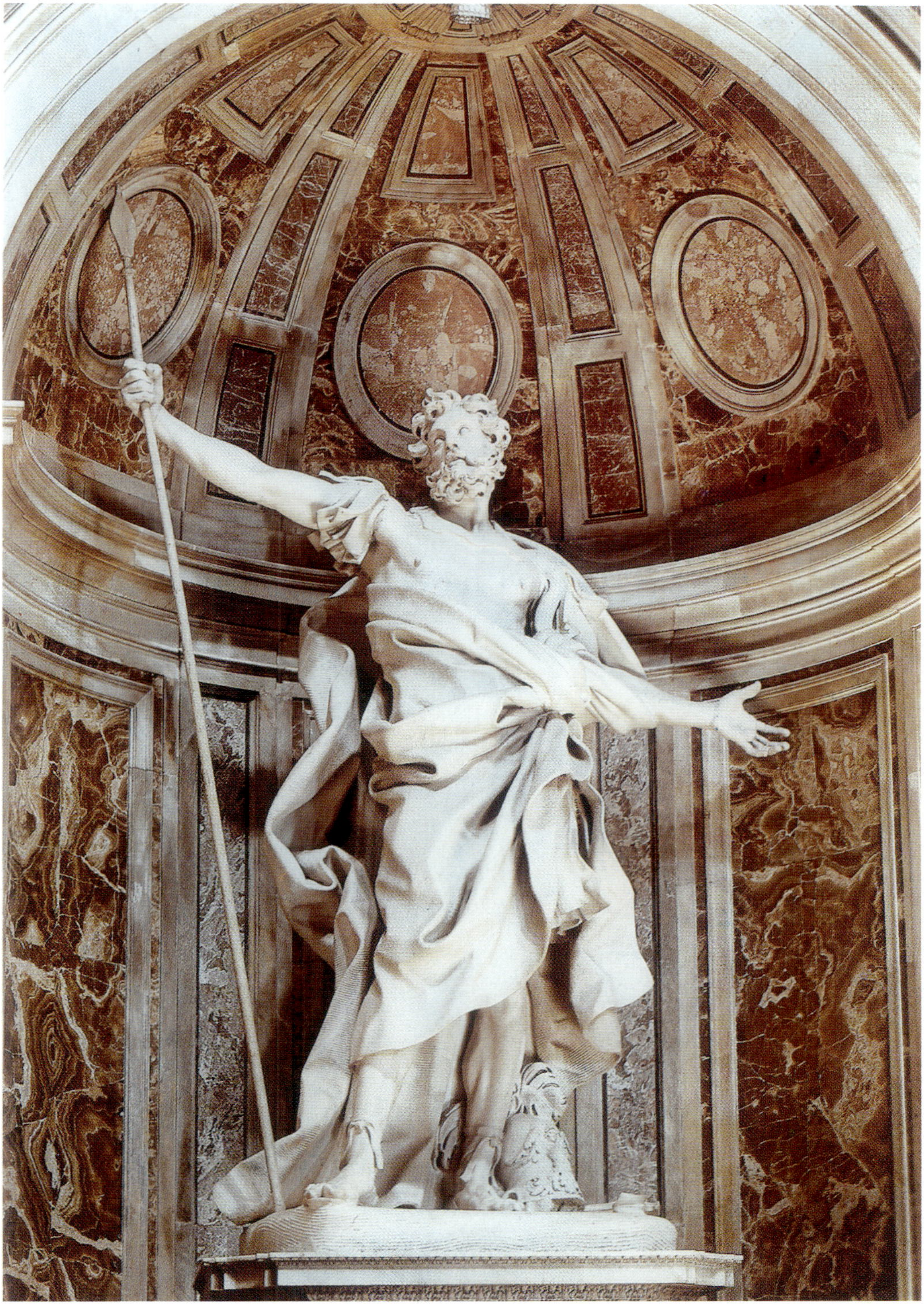

St. Longinus (1629-1638), marble. Vatican City, Basilica of St. Peter

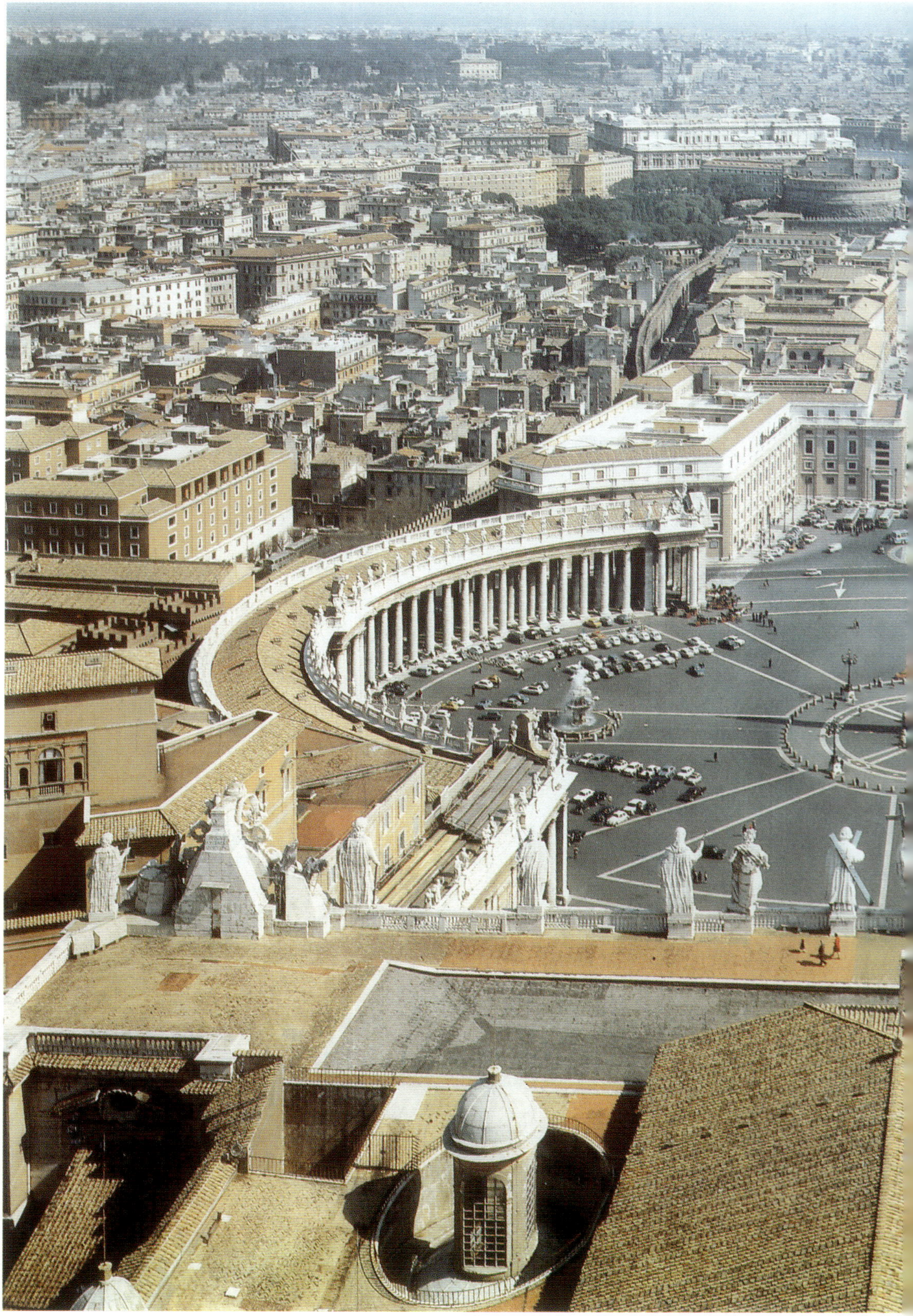

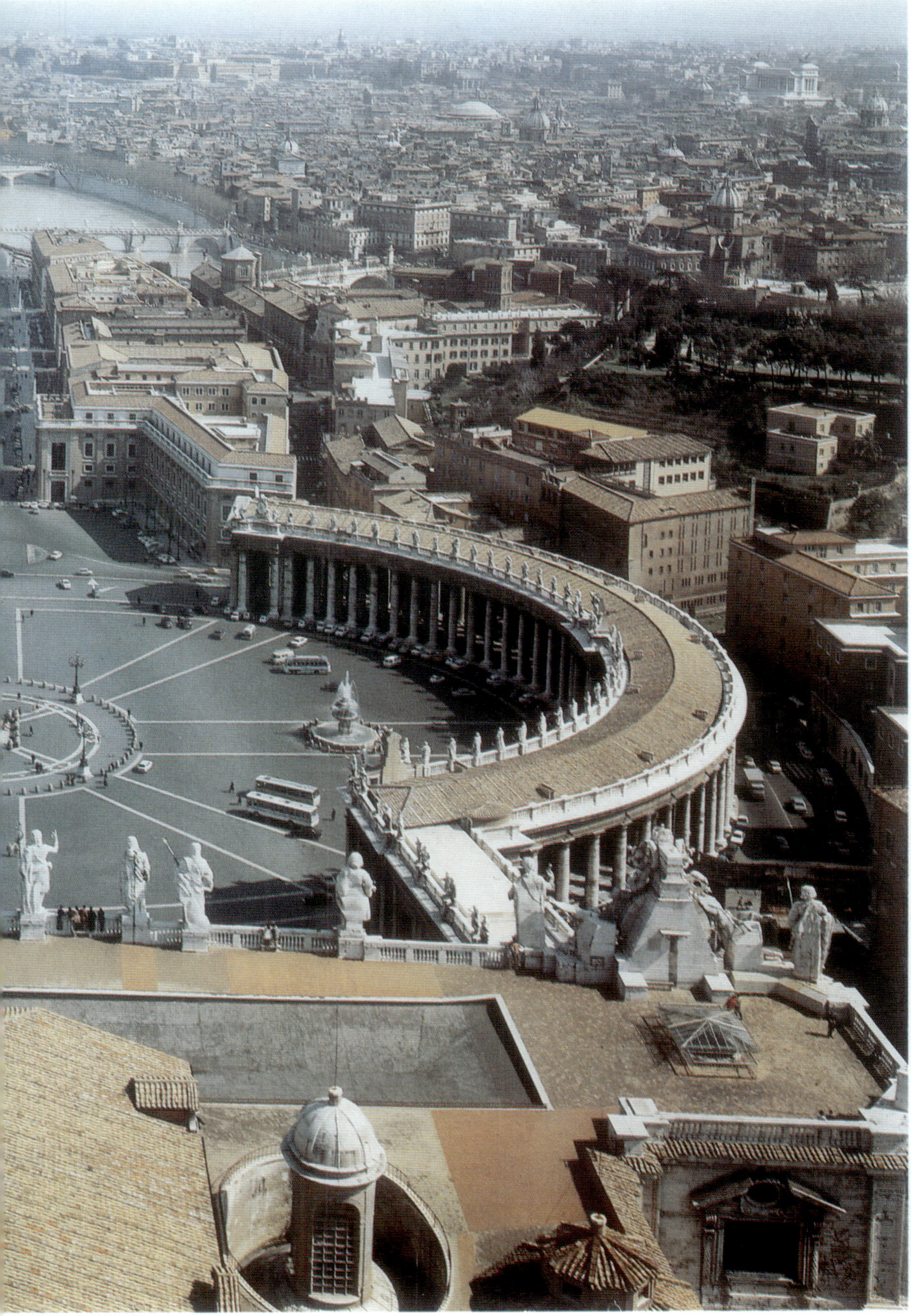

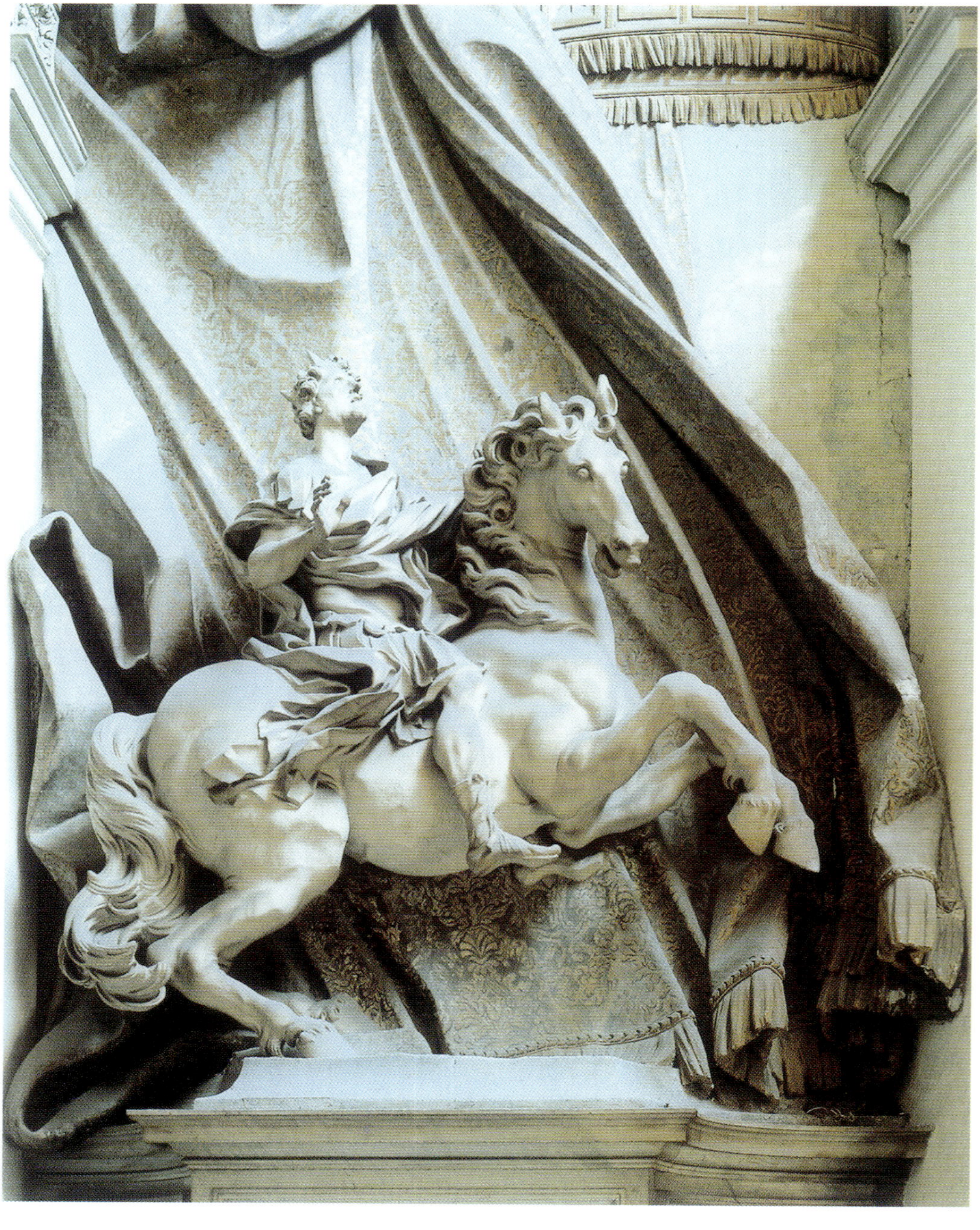

Constantine (1654-1670), marble. Vatican City, Basilica of St. Peter

Previous page:
St. Peter's square. Vatican City

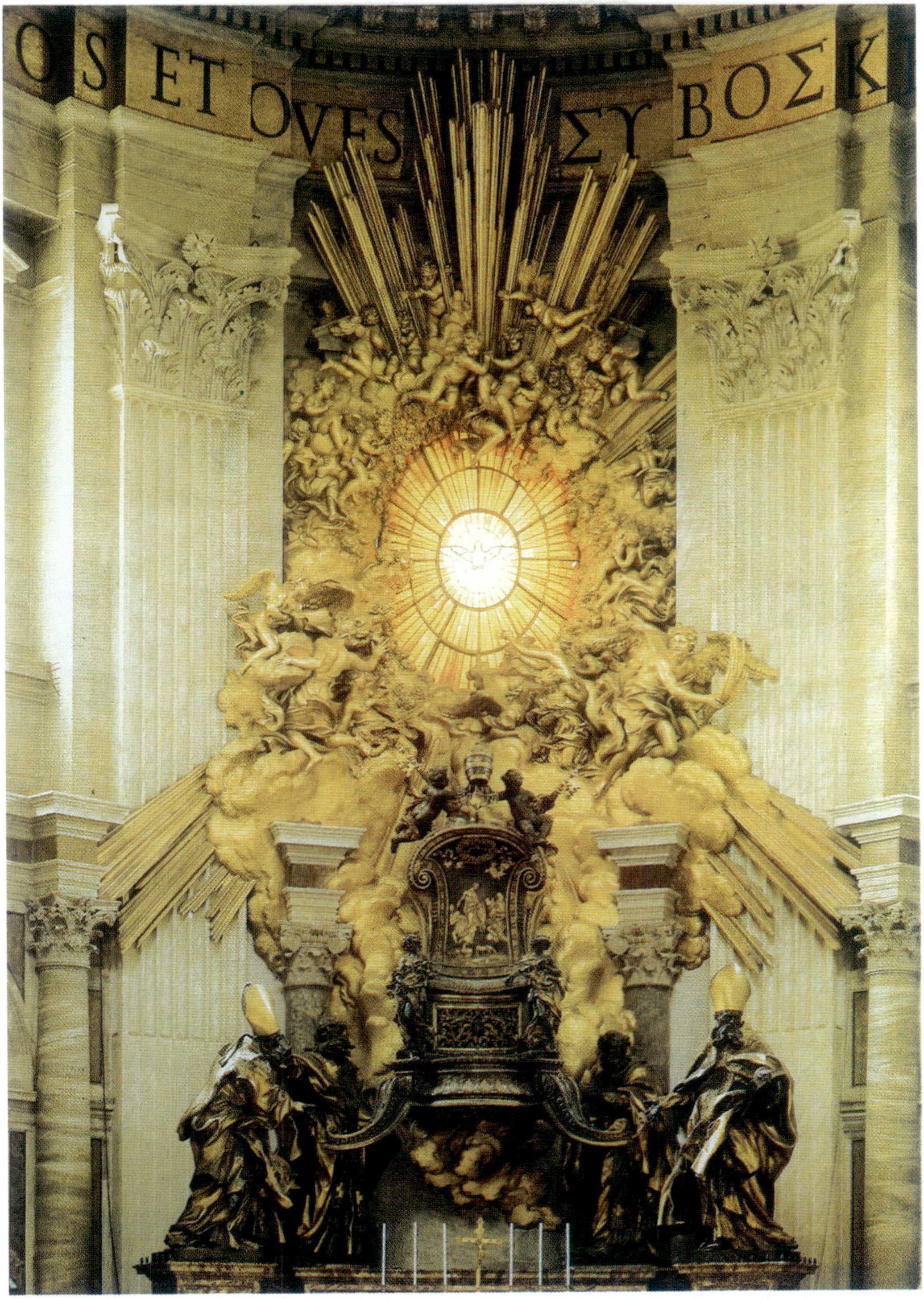

Cathedra of St. Peter (1657-1666), marble, bronze, stucco.
Vatican City, Basilica of St. Peter

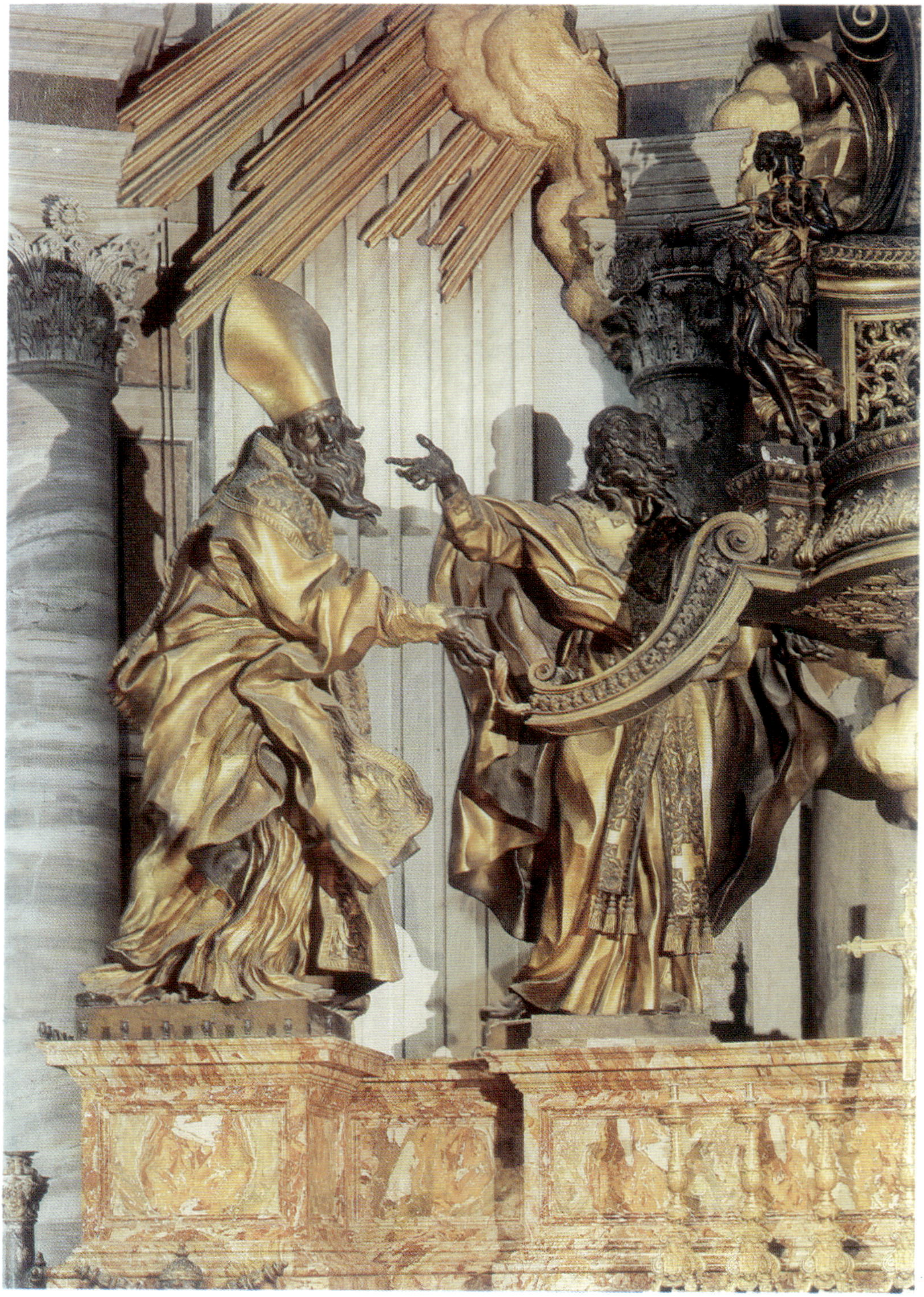

Cathedra of St. Peter, detail (1657-1666), marble, bronze, stucco.
Vatican City, Basilica of St. Peter

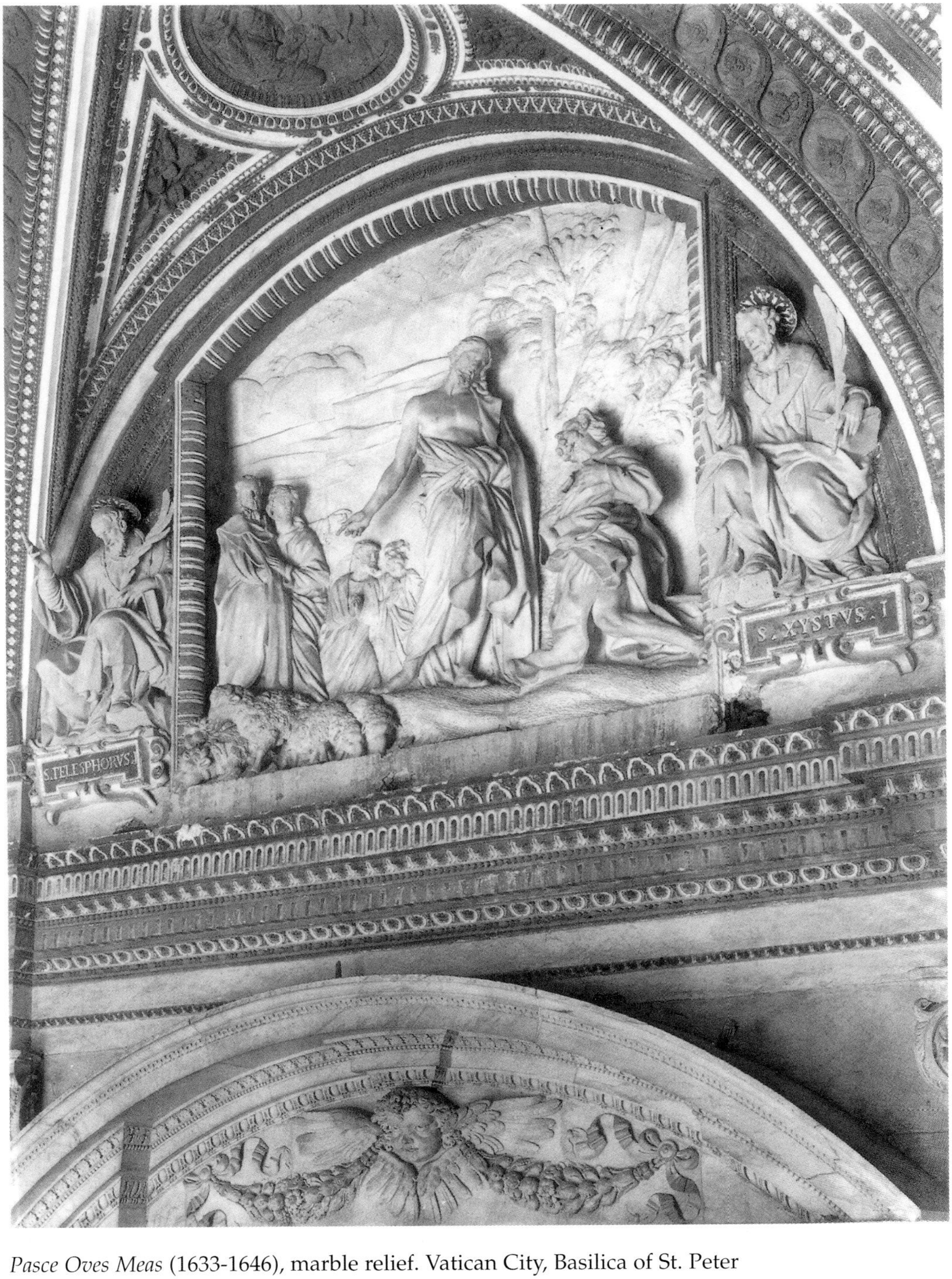

Pasce Oves Meas (1633-1646), marble relief. Vatican City, Basilica of St. Peter

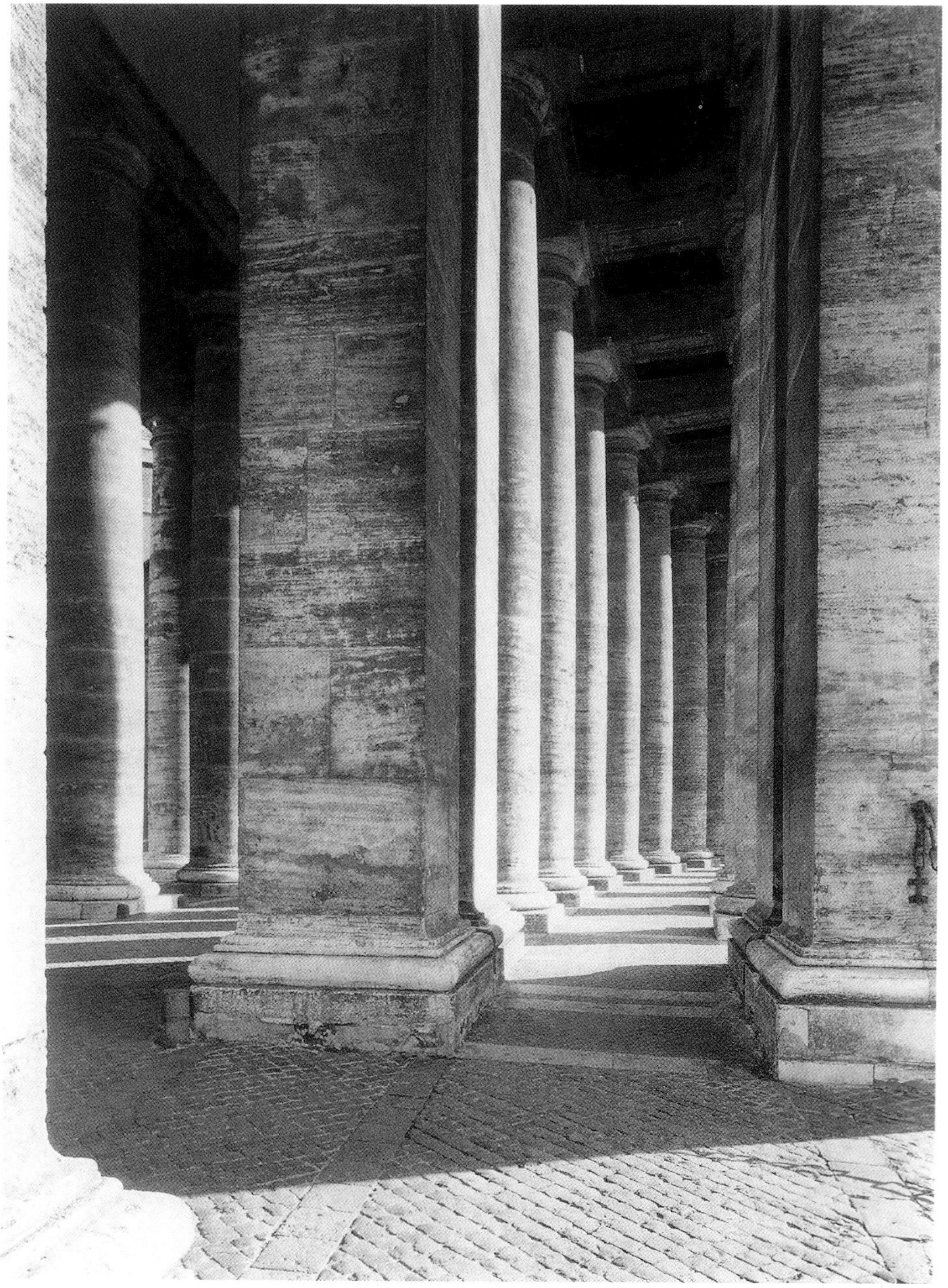

Colonnade (1656-1667). Vatican City, St. Peter's square

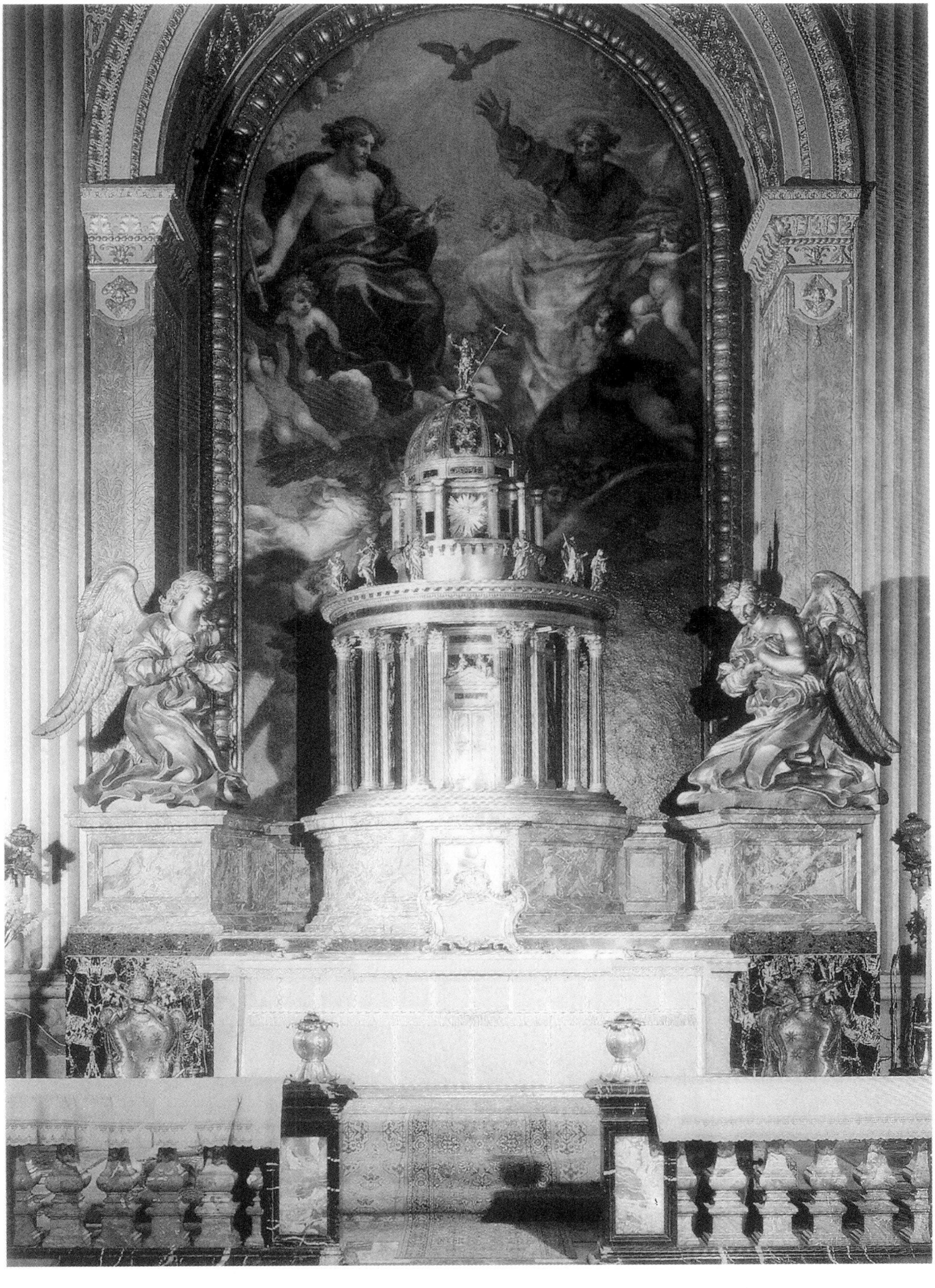

Altar of the Sacrament (1673-1674), bronze and marble. Vatican City, Basilica of St. Peter

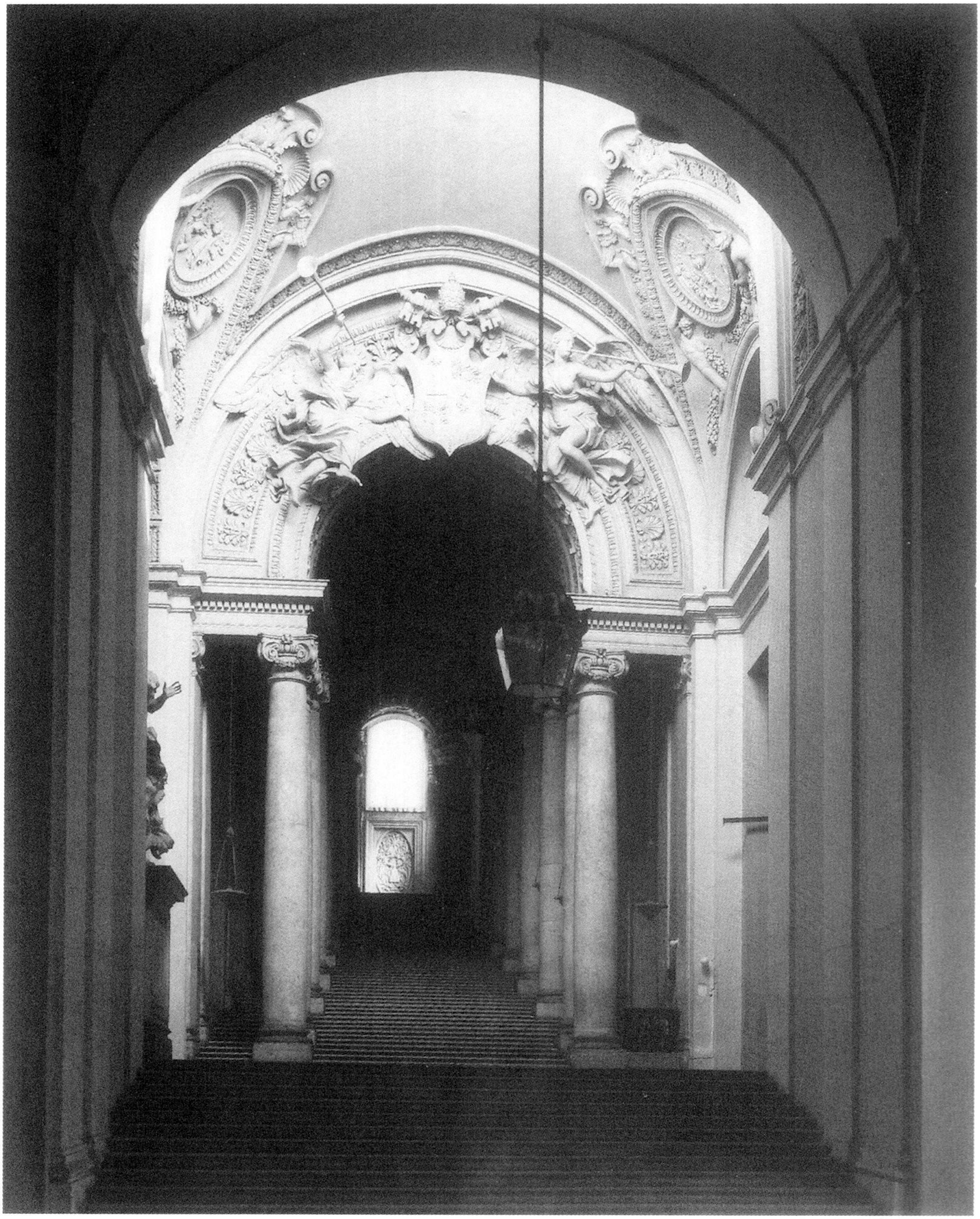

Scala Regia (1664). Vatican City, Vatican Palace

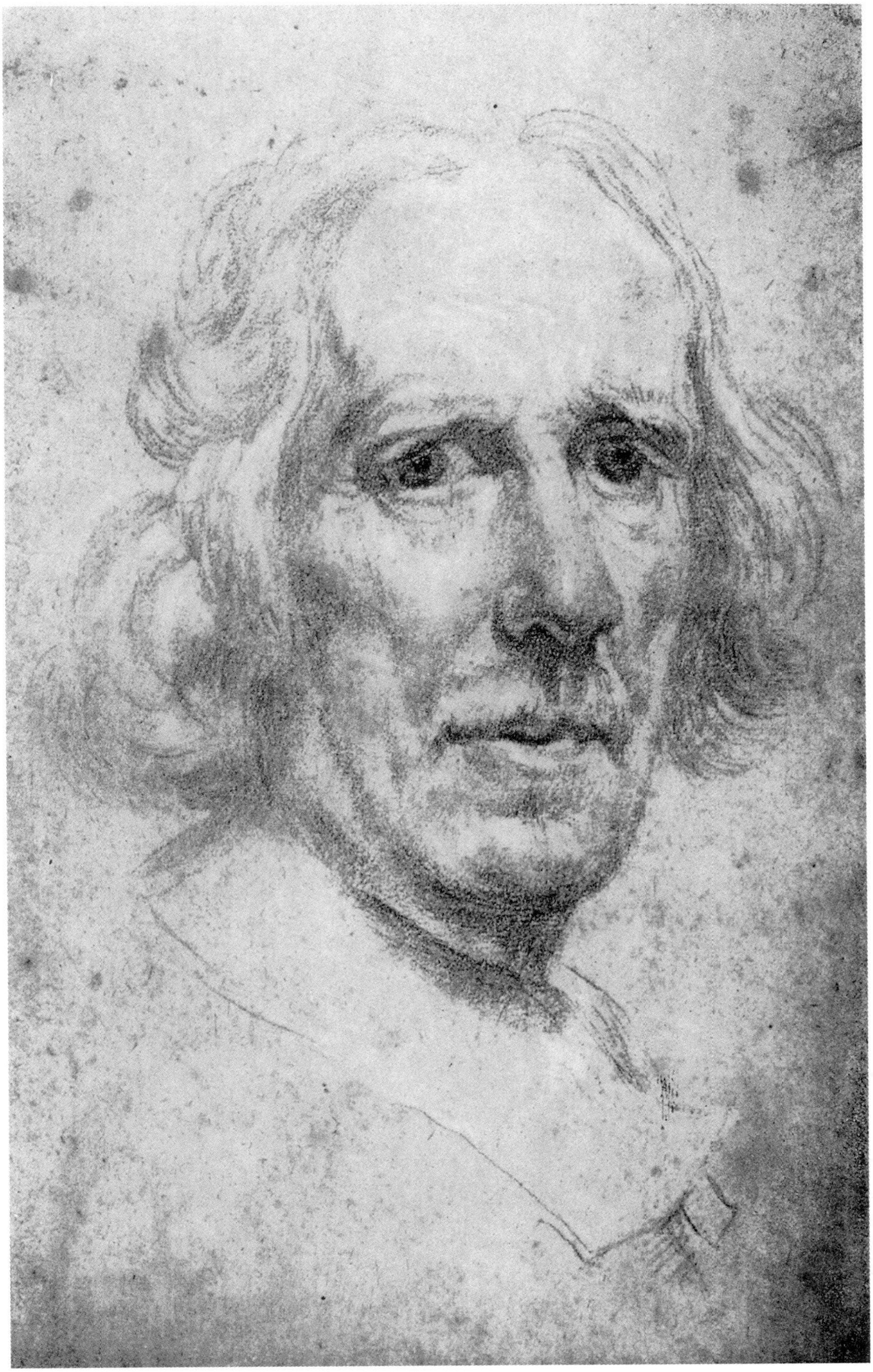

Self-portrait as an old man (1665). Windsor Castle, The Royal Collection

Index of works

Rome, Piazza Barberini
41 *Fontana delle Api,* 1644

Rome, Church of Santa Maria della Vittoria
42 *The Cornaro Family, 1645-1652*
45 *Ecstasy of St. Teresa,* 1645-1652

Rome, Galleria Doria Pamphili
46 *Innocent X,* 1647 ca.

Rome, Piazza Navona
47 *Four Rivers Fountain,* 1648-1651

Modena, Museo Estense
50 *Francesco I d'Este,* 1650-1651

Rome, Church of Santa Maria del Popolo
51 *Daniel,* 1655-1657
52 *Habakkuk,* 1655-1657

Rome, Church of Sant'Andrea al Quirinale
53 *Cupola,* 1658-1665
54 *Facade,* 1658-1665

Siena, Cathedral
55 *Mary Magdalen,* 1661
56 *St. Jerome,* 1663

Rome, Palazzo Odescalchi
57 *Facade,* 1665

Rome, Palazzo della Minerva
58 *Elephant,* 1666-1667

Rome, Church of Sant'Andrea delle Fratte
59 *Angel with crown of thorns,* 1667-1669
60 *Angel with scroll,* 1667-1669

Rome, Basilica of Santa Maria Maggiore
4 *Apse* (exterior), 1669

Rome, Ponte Sant'Angelo
61 *Angel with scroll* (copy by Cartari), 1669-1671

Rome, Church of San Francesco a Ripa
62 *Blessed Ludovica Albertoni,* 1671-1674

Rome, Church of San Lorenzo in Lucina
63 *Gabriele Fonseca,* 1668-1675

Basilica of St. Peter and Vatican
65 *Baldacchino,* 1624-1633
66 *Tomb of Urban VIII,* 1628-1647
67 *St. Longinus,* 1629-1638
64 *Tomb of countess Matilde,* 1633-1637
73 *Pasce Oves Meas,* 1633-1646
70 *Constantine,* 1654-1670
68 *St. Peter's square,*
74 *Colonnade,* 1656-1667
71 *Cathedra of St. Peter,* 1657-1666
76 *Scala Regia,* 1664
75 *Altar of the Sacrament,* 1673-1674

Windsor Castle
77 *Self-portrait as an old man,* 1665 ca.

Photographic references:
Alinari-Anderson Photographic archive: pp. 32, 46, 64, 73.
Fratelli Palombi Photographic archive: pp. 6, 16, 77.
Scala Photographic archive: pp. 6, 20, 21, 24, 34, 35, 40, 42, 43, 50, 53, 55, 56, 65, 66, 67, 68, 69, 70, 71, 72, 74, 75, 76.
Vasari Photographic Studio: pp. 4, 5, 9, 10, 11, 12, 13, 14, 15, 17, 18, 19, 22, 23, 25, 26, 27, 28, 29, 30, 31, 33, 36, 37, 38, 39, 41, 44, 45, 47, 48, 49, 51, 52, 54, 57, 58, 59, 60, 61, 62, 63.

Print:
Fratelli Palombi S.r.l.
Via dei Gracchi, 181/187 - 00192 Roma
October 2001